CREEKSIDE TALES

Life on the East Coast of England

ROBERT SIMPER.

Published by Creekside Publishing

ISBN 0 9538506 5 X
Copyright Robert Simper 2004
Printed by Lavenham Press Ltd
Lavenham, Suffolk

Rivers & Sands of the Thames approaches
Lil

Lowestoft

Southwold

River Waveney

River Blyth

River Alde

River Ore

Snape

Thorpeness
Aldeburgh

River Deben

River Gipping

Butley

Orford

Orford Ness

Melton
Woodbridge
Eyke
Sutton Hoo
Shottisham
Ramsholt

Orford Haven
Shingle Street
Bawdsey Ferry

Waldringfield
Hemley

Ipswich

River Orwell

Pinmill

Felixstowe

Woodbridge Haven
Felixstowe Ferry

River Stour

Mistley

Harwich

Great Oakley

Colchester
Wivenhoe
Alresford
Brightlingsea
St Osyth

River Colne

Walton-on-the-Naze

River Blackwater

Mersea Island

Jaywick
Clacton-on-sea

Wallet

East Swin

Tollesbury

Spitway

Barrow Deep

Black Deep

Maldon
Northey
Island
Osea
Island

Dengie Flat

River Crouch

Burnham
-on-Crouch

River Roach
Foulness
Island

Maplin Sands

West Swin

Leigh-on-Sea
Southend
-on-sea

Canvey Is.

+ Red Sand Tower

Red Sand

Middle
Sand

River Thames

Hoo

Queenborough

Isle of Sheppey

North
Foreland

River Medway
Rochester

The Swale

Whitstable

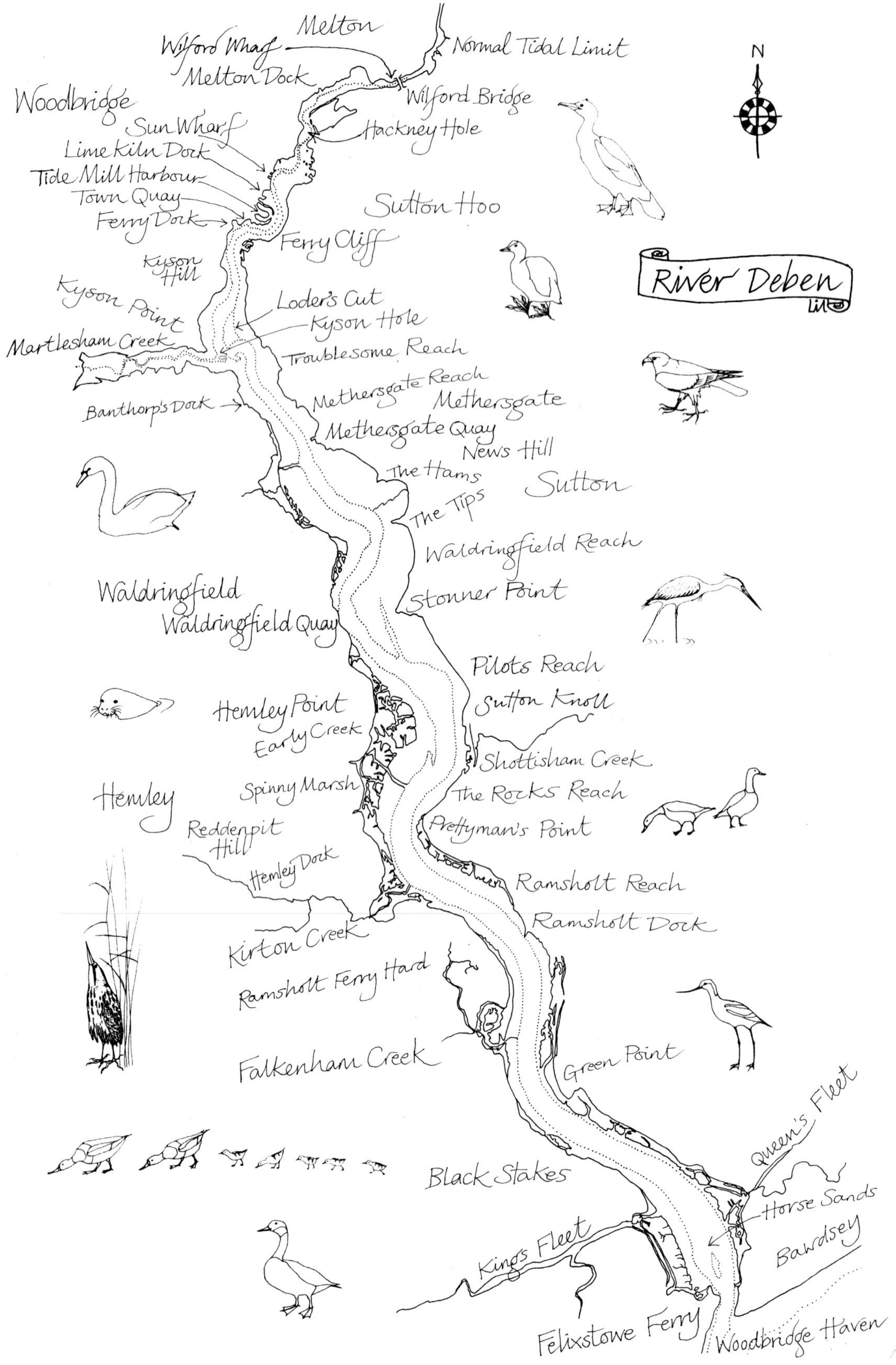

Melton

Wilford Wharf

Melton Dock

Normal Tidal Limit

Woodbridge

Sun Wharf

Lime Kiln Dock

Tide Mill Harbour

Town Quay

Ferry Dock

Wilford Bridge

Hackney Hole

Sutton Hoo

Ferry Cliff

Kyson Hill

Kyson Point

Loder's Cut

Kyson Hole

Martlesham Creek

Troublesome Reach

Banthorp's Dock

Methersgate Reach

Methersgate

Methersgate Quay

News Hill

The Hams

The Tips

Sutton

Waldringfield Reach

Stonner Point

Waldringfield

Waldringfield Quay

River Deben

Pilots Reach

Hemley Point

Early Creek

Sutton Knoll

Shottisham Creek

The Rocks Reach

Hemley

Spinny Marsh

Prettyman's Point

Reddenpit Hill

Hemley Dock

Ramsholt Reach

Ramsholt Dock

Kirton Creek

Ramsholt Ferry Hard

Falkenham Creek

Green Point

Queen's Fleet

Black Stakes

Horse Sands

Bawdsey

King's Fleet

Felixstowe Ferry

Woodbridge Haven

N

Contents

Introduction

I could hear the rain hitting the windowpane behind me with such force that when I looked through the window at the river it was almost blotted out from view. Since I have never mastered the art of sitting still and doing nothing, I started to jot down memories of living in an isolated cottage by a creek for forty-five years. Your environment shapes your attitudes and experiences. How should I shape such a series of rural and maritime recollections? Certainly an explanation as to why we have spent a lifetime in one place. My son Jonathan came in and made suggestions to the basic format while my daughter Caroline Southernwood, who teaches design, said, 'it must be different to your maritime history books'. My wife Pearl waited until she started editing before she helped to shape the end result. The result is personal experiences, set against the background of the creeks and rivers of the East Coast.

I have long tried to make some kind of record of the changing pattern of events around the Thames Estuary. The earliest attempt here is the drawing I did of the wreck of the schooner *Rudolf* at Shingle Street in about 1953.

Acknowledgements

To bring the atmosphere of the East Coast creeks to life we enlisted the help of environmental artist Lil Tudor Craig. In 1984, when Lil bought the 68ft *2605* her boating experience had been limited to hiring a paddleboat, as a child, on Southwold Boating Pond. Over the next twelve years Lil, with her partner Tony, lived aboard the *2605* at Melton and made voyages to all the East Coast Rivers. They also took out parties of divers on treasure hunting explorations in the Thames Estuary. The *2605,* one of eighty-nine Type III "Hants and Dorset" high speed Air Sea Rescue launches was built in 1943. These were designed by George Selman and built by the British Powerboat Co for the RAF to rescue airmen who ditched into the sea. Many high-speed motor launches, of various types, were built during the war and their light double diagonal construction was only expected to last for the 'duration of the war'. However many have lasted far longer.

After the war a colony of 'Little Ships' became houseboats on the Deben at Melton. Of these the *MGB 60* was a houseboat at Sun Wharf, Woodbridge from 1948 until she was towed to Lowestoft in 1999. After three years of rebuilding for preservation the *MGB 60* was totally destroyed in the Newson Boatyard fire in 2004. Meanwhile Lil had sold the *2605* and moved on to the 62ft motorboat *Sunfleet*, ex-Port of London Authority motorboat Gunfleet. Later the *Sunfleet* was moved to Newhaven, Sussex, but Lil has since returned to live in Suffolk.

My thanks go to other people who have supplied material, most of whom are mentioned in the text. Derek Sederman gave me details about Abbotsholme School. Gerrard Swift talked to me about barges on the Blackwater. As well as doing the drawings, Lil Tudor-Craig kindly read the text and made corrections.

Jonathan, Pearl or myself took most photographs but Rosemary Hoppitt took the photographs in the British Museum. Thanks to Archant Norfolk for the photograph of Southwold and to Janet Harber who kindly let me have an aerial view of the River Deben entrance.

RS.
Ramsholt 2004

Bawdsey Ferry.

Snape Maltings.

The Creek.

Chapter One

Almost an Education

They say that wherever you live you only have just two homes in your life. Where you grow up and the place that your children grow up, those two you will always think of as 'home'. Certainly things you do when you are young stay with you for the rest of your life; at least that has been my experience. From about 1946 I was going out on the River Deben and when I was old enough was allowed to go on trawling trips at night. This was in the open Suffolk beach boat *Lassie,* which was owned by John Garrard. My imagination must have been stirred by a night trip trawling because, back at school, in about 1952, I did a painting of her and Mr Heath thought it good enough to be put up on the Art Room wall. There was the *Lassie,* greyer than the night, having her trawl hauled. In the background was The Creek with The Cottage just over the river wall. I had no idea that this would be the spot where, in the not so distant future, I was going to go and live and spend most of my life.

The *Mary Amelia* on her mooring near The Cottage.

I have tried to remember my exact first memory of the Suffolk River. I know that I was taken for picnics on the beach of the Deben, as a young child, because of photographs. This was some time before World War II. My mother tells me that we once went on a pleasure boat from Felixstowe beach, near the pier, up the River Orwell to Pin Mill to see the ships unloading wheat. As the upper reaches of the Orwell were still shallow, before dredging, the barges took the wheat up to the Ipswich mills. I dearly wish I could remember seeing the barges break away from the ships and hoisting their topsails to run up-river.

I do remember going in search of winkles with the Garrard family in about 1943. We went down to Ramsholt Dock, then a deserted barge quay at the end of a muddy track by the River Deben, and walked along the river wall and through a reed bed in search of winkles. I don't remember the out-come of this adventure; just fighting my way through the reeds and suddenly coming out to see the grey ooze mud with the evening light on the tidal waters beyond. This was during the War and the river was, strictly speaking, closed to the public, but I was fascinated by the grey still waters of the estuary.

This slight memory of a far off time has stayed with me. Another early memory of the nineteen-forties came flooding back when Pearl and I got out of the car at the local school and returned to the hall of my first school. A brisk breeze was blowing straight from the North Sea and inside there was the high-pitched hum of excited children's voices. We went into the main hall and sat down, waiting to see our grandson Harry in the Bawdsey School Nativity play. I was completely disoriented, Pearl quietly whispered that we were sitting on chairs for small children, but it was more than that. I had left this school, I think in 1944, fifty–eight years before, and had not been back into the school since then.

The room suddenly seemed a lot smaller, especially sitting on those little chairs. Everything had altered; the gardens where we had attempted to grow vegetables had become a sports field. New classrooms had been built over the girl's playground and the whole school had become a lot larger. No longer did everyone speak in a Suffolk voice, but there were still the same young excited faces.

Most village schools in the area had been closed, but Bawdsey School only existed because of an administrative blunder in the nineteen-sixties. At that time the vogue for closing small rural schools was just starting and Bawdsey did not have a large enough population to support its own school. However someone in London looked at the situation and ruled that because of RAF Bawdsey personnel and the large radar station that was a vital part of the Cold War, Bawdsey School should stay open. However the faraway administrators had not known that the Married Quarters for RAF Bawdsey were in fact in the neighbouring, larger village of Alderton. So Alderton School, which had more children, was closed and the smaller Bawdsey School enlarged.

I am not sure how old I was when I started at Bawdsey School, but I do remember the first day vividly. In rural Suffolk during World War II there was no pre-school training. The school was at the opposite end of the village from where we lived on a remote farm and I don't remember having ever seen it before the first day of term. My mother took me to the school door, pushed me in and quickly cycled off. I walked apprehensively into the tiny cloakroom and was shown where to hang my coat by a teacher.

I stood in silence with a small group of children when the door was flung open and a harassed-looking woman dragged a small boy in, who was fighting and screaming. This small boy obviously did not wish to begin the first steps towards adulthood. There was a shouting match and then the distraught young mother fled out of the door, leaving a teacher holding the very reluctant pupil. All the small children looked at each other in terror, wondering if school life was always like this.

In fact we went into the large school hall, the same room that I had returned to over fifty years later, where there were lines of heavy wooden and iron desks. The infants sat in the desks near the door and as they grew older they were moved across the hall.

The whole school was looked after by one teacher who sat at a large desk at the front, near the coke stove. I don't remembered discipline being particularly tough, but we were all very well behaved. I am told now that the teacher's name was Mrs Crane, but I don't remember anything about her. The fact that the school failed to teach me very much is probably my fault, but I think it was a happy time. We small boys were all very excited by the War that was going on above and around us. Boys came to school with bits of shell and aircraft.

Once small bombs hit the schoolhouse and because of the damage we had a few days off. I was pleased about that, but I was very worried, well to be honest terrified, when we had to put gas masks on. The tiny perspex window steamed up quickly when I started breathing in it and I was very relieved when I was allowed to take it off.

A worse experience was going into the school air raid shelter. This was a low iron box, I think it was known as an Anderson shelter, which was in a lobby at the far end of the hall. Fortunately most of the air raids were during darkness and the bombers were usually going over looking for the towns, but once in the middle of the day we were all ordered to crawl into the shelters. We sat inside, bent over, crammed together. There was hardly room to breathe. Goodness knows what would have happened if a bomb had actually hit the school. Luckily none did.

From Bawdsey School my parents moved me on to a small boarding school in Ipswich. School is a rehearsal for real life; powerful personalities will seek to gain a dominant role. I survived quite well at boarding school, but small boys are very unforgiving and the weak did get bullied. To survive in the basic jungle of boarding school life I needed to be good at something. I started to act out great battles with toys on the desktop and boys would gather around to follow the story. This led on to boys saying, after lights out in the dormitory, 'come on Simper tell us a story.' These were mostly in the same vein as 'Dick Barton, Special Agent'; a highly imaginative radio programme which was then immensely popular with young boys. My story telling earned me respect from both the boys and, I found out later, from the masters. After 'lights out' there was supposed to be a 'no talking' rule and the master in charge listened at the door to make sure that we were not plotting some great mischief. The masters worked out that if I was heard telling some unlikely yarn then there were not going to be any problems and they could return to the safety of the staff room. We used to hear laughter coming from the Staff Common Room and speculate about the type of wild parties that might have gone on in there.

After attending this Prep school my parents had intended to send me to Framlingham College, the usual place for local farmers to send their sons. Most farmers' sons were good all round outdoor types who loved sport. I hated sport and pleaded not to be sent there. To my surprise my parents listened to my request, or perhaps they did not wish my lack of sporting ability to show them up in front of the whole district. They were told about this school called Abbotsholme, in Staffordshire, which had a farm where some of the boys could work instead of taking up sports. I was not thrilled at the prospect of being sent a long way from my beloved home on the coast, but it sounded better than anywhere that involved team sports. Unfortunately Abbotsholme was already full up, but the Governors had started another over-spill school, Doveleys, on the other side of the village of Rocester. At the age of eleven I was deposited in the English Midlands and became a stranger in a strange county.

Abbotsholme had been the creation of several fairly eccentric schoolmasters and was an attempt to come up with an alternative to the English nineteenth century public school. In the book of the school's history there was not a single photograph of a sporting activity. There are photographs of boys making hay in 1894 and building a henhouse and a boathouse. There are accounts of boys driving cattle to Uttoxeter market and breeding ferrets to catch rats around the hen house. Good rural stuff, but by the time I arrived at Doveleys it was a far more conventional teaching establishment. However, the spirit of the early pioneers was strong enough to make it 'different'.

Doveleys was an attractive nineteenth century country house built by a successful industrialist in a beautiful rural valley overlooking the River Dove. On the other side of the river was the Ashbourne to Uttoxeter railway line along which a tiny locomotive, pulling two carriages, steamed past several times a day in a cloud of black smoke. On our 'Days Out', we were allowed to go and cycle around the district. I used to cycle down to Ellastone Station with Watson and watch the strange ritual of passing the ring. The train had to stop, and could not go on up the line until the stationmaster had signalled the 'all cleared ahead' by passing over the ring.

Indeed Doveleys had once had its own railway system. The industrialist, who built Doveleys, had a pet idea that the world could be opened up by narrow gauge railways, so he had one constructed in his grounds. I once saw a television documentary where one of his little railways was still operating in the foothills of India. Sadly his successors, pushed for cash, had torn up and sold most of the Doveleys track, shortly before the place became a school, but a tiny section had survived. On 'Outdoor Activities' afternoons we boys were detailed to load the little trucks with firewood and push them up to the back door where they were unloaded for the school fires. Doveleys did not actually have the promised farm, instead we had Outdoor Activities, which meant maintaining the school grounds. Cutting down trees in the woods (my school axe is still my most treasured personal possession) was something I loved and I was very happy with the free and easy life.

Some days we had the 'Pet Club' instead of sport. My friend on the very rural side was Howard Harris. His father was a successful shopkeeper in Cheadle and while having Sunday lunch there one day he announced that the first of his sons to become a doctor would be given £1000. Howard was not in the least interested; he just wanted to be a farmer.

At the weekends we cycled up into the hills above Ashbourne where some of Howard's relations were still farming. They spoke a dialect which had very little to do with Standard English and were always immensely kind to us. The afternoons always ended in a cottage beside the road where Mrs Robottom, the family's grandmother, lived. Every time we went there she was very careful to tell me that the proper way to pronounce her name was Ro-bo-tham. We used to sit around her coal-burning range while she reminisced with 'our Howard' about life on the farm back in the Victorian era. She talked about the day when they were milking in the stone byre when it suddenly started to rain and the men all rushed out to get the hay in. She had been left to hand milk all the cows.

Howard and I cornered the market in rhubarb. We used to go around the Doveleys' park with buckets and scoop up the cow muck and with this organic technology grew some amazingly good rhubarb. We also kept chickens and some eggs we sold or we had 'fry ups' over a fire in the woods. I became very keen on a breed of bantams known as Indian Game, lovely birds, but they laid remarkably few eggs. Howard once got the inside information that a prize cockerel was for sale. We cycled off, at speed, to purchase the bird from a terraced house near the bridge just before Ashbourne. Behind the houses were pigeon lofts and chicken runs, a serious world for bird fanciers.

The Indian Game breeder would not accept payment. Saying that when the birds bred I should return with several hens. A fair deal, but it has always been on my conscience because I left school and returned to Suffolk long before my hens laid any eggs.

I don't remember any of the masters taking any interest in the Pet Club or ever coming near it. Nor did anyone ever enquire where we went on our cycle rides, although we were supposed to write our destination on a board before we left.

Doveleys was intended to turn out boys that 'did their own thing' in an age when most people still thought that going into the army was good for young men, because of the enforced discipline. If anything, Doveleys suffered from a lack of discipline, but there were strong army influences. Several of the young masters had fought in World War II and at meal times they passed on army slang. I still think of a lavatory as being 'The bog'. Best of all, on Saturday evenings we did 'commando raids'. We blacked up our faces and one 'unit' defended the sewage works while the rest attacked. The defenders had torches and if they called out your name you were 'dead'. I remember a sharp fight in the rhododendrons with a very angry boy because I refused to 'die' when my name was called out. I was determined to take the position, come hell or high water.

The 'activity runs' around the school grounds must also have been affected by the army because they looked suspiciously like commando courses. Once in the depth of winter the course included fording the River Dove to a small island. With the master shouting encouragement we hung on to a piece of rope and the brown swirling water came up to our chests as we fought our way across. Several small boys were scared out of their wits, but none, surprisingly, were drowned. Our mothers would probably have been horrified and any teacher would probably have been sacked on the spot today for sending boys off on these 'near death' experiences. Most of us, on the other hand, rather enjoyed them.

Don't get me wrong about Doveleys, we were not being encouraged to be part of an organized army unit, rather as independent guerrilla fighters. It was my parents who were most puzzled by this philosophy. Someone had told them that boarding schools always taught boys to play cricket with a straight bat. In spite of the undoubted expense for my education, I avoided cricket like the plague. Once, with Peter Barton and Roger Danby, we went canoeing on the River Dove. With three of us in a one-man canoe it turned over while shooting the rapids. After fighting our way out, Roger swam downsteam to get the canoe and paddled back, then we turned up for cricket soaking wet. The master in charge seemed surprisingly unmoved by the late arrival of three soaking wet boys. He made us play the game as we were. I remember being very cold. It never occurred to me that this could have been remedied by putting some effort into the game and running about! At least our late arrival had reduced the amount of time we had to take part in the tedious game.

The only time I really ran with enthusiasm on the sports field was when the full time whistle had gone. It was magic in my ears and I ran back as hard as I could to the changing rooms. The idea was to get there before the master arrived to enforce me to have a shower. The Doveleys' showers were not a technical success; the water was either very hot or very cold and one dashed in and out making the best of the situation. My great aim was to get dressed and vanish into the school library, a haven of peace and quiet.

Doveleys had only been going a short while and the library was not very large. After World War II the Labour Government had brought in high taxation that destroyed the country house system and hundreds of old houses were pulled down and their contents auctioned off cheaply. Someone, probably the Governor, Captain Wenner, must have been to a country house sale and acquired the brown leather-bound Victorian books that lined the Doveley's library. Our library must have looked impressive to visiting parents, but it was not a place to develop progressive-thinking minds. I read everything in sight and became an extremely good source of useless facts. For instance I have a fair knowledge of the political run-up to the Boer War, but am totally unable to achieve simple things like putting flat-pack furniture together. There is nothing more useless on this planet than a cupboard with drawers that will not fit!

To me the Library was heaven, I spent hours reading old leather bound copies of *Punch*. There were other books, already fifty years out of date, about travel and settlers in the Empire. I devoured them all and acquired a thoroughly good grounding in the history of Victorian Britain. When I started writing books I rarely had to look up details about that period. I felt I had almost lived through it.

Most of the way we behave is genetic, we are simply a repeat of our ancestors, but we never quite know which one. On top of that there are 'influences from early life'. The strongest personality at Doveleys was undoubtedly Hugh Maw, a Quaker who had refused to go into the army. Which was good news for Britain's enemies, because he was a tough man and well able to fight for any cause he believed in.

Then there was Lewis Heath, our art teacher, who, since I poured out a series of dramatic seascapes and shipwrecks, allowed me to join the elite band allowed to use the Art Room in their spare time. Mr Heath loved making little jokes, which were never funny. The chief one was that his father was Ted Heath, the popular bandleader. 'Then why aren't you good at music, Sir?' We muttered, never too loudly, because Mr Heath was very quick to cut you down to size.

Music was my personal Waterloo, I could not sing or 'hold a tune'. Once the music master, Ken Broun, an elderly man we called 'Bromas the Bear', got me to stand in front of the class and clap in time while he played the piano. He was exasperated and said 'Simper, you sound just like a cow relieving itself. Sit down and for goodness sake stop talking'.

Not good for my morale, but probably an accurate description. Bromas was a kindly old man, coasting along. He would have liked to have retired early, but he had married a younger woman and started another family. Sometimes he got bored and drifted off talking about the great romances in his life. He had obviously been a real dandy back in the nineteen-twenties, his tired old eyes would light up when he talked of the girls he had met at parties. We pressed for more details, but never got them.

He implored me to get at least some of my Latin tenses correct. I replied that I didn't think I would ever need Latin. Could I please switch to the German class? I was much attracted by the stylish way the German alphabet was written.

'Simper' he said very firmly with a great deal of worldly wisdom, 'when you go through life you will find Latin useful at every turn.'

I might have been a better person if I had known Latin, but I can honestly say I have never once had a real need for it. But I do remember these men and the views on life they gave us.

My interest in foreign countries and different cultures was possibly started off because there were so many boys from overseas. I slept between two Indian boys from Uganda, East Africa, and I have often wondered what had become of them when they were thrown out of their country. Then we always had at least one French teacher from the exchange with L'Ecole des Roches in Normandy. The exchange teacher we all remembered with most affection was a rather pretty Swiss lady called Miss Switzer. On hot summer days she used to appear in lovely see-through blouses. Although matron was heard muttering disapprovingly, Miss Switzer's arrival in the dining room sent an electric current through all the boys and most of the masters. Our cloistered life style meant that the faint glimpse of a real bra was even more exciting than the topless tribal photographs in the *National Geographic Magazine.*

That summer many boys suddenly became interested in the French language, and used to stand very close to Miss Switzer while asking for a translation of various obscure words which required a long explanation. The Headmaster, Leslie Stephens, is reputed to have taken Miss Switzer aside and suggested that she wore something more appropriate for a Boys Boarding School.

This was one of his more sensible moves. Leslie Stephens, and his always-busy wife Dido, were very hard working, but this ambitious couple were very seriously lacking in what today would have been called 'people skills'.

The staff were appalled when it became known that one of the parents who complained about their son's lack of progress were told abruptly, 'You can't make a silk purse out of a sow's ear'.

Without delay the parents arranged for their son's belongings to be loaded into their car and the family departed, never to be seen again. What was worse, they clearly spread the idea to other parents of their acquaintance. The Stephens departed to West Buckland School and it is probable that they were happier at a more traditional boarding school. Our school's liberal approach needed a lot of imagination to make it work; we were supposed to play games purely for the joy of taking part. This meant that our football team was soundly thrashed on many occasions. Sport really does not mean anything, but in real life a winning team is seen as a marker that your tribe is successful.

Gradually the class sizes began to get smaller and an unpleasant relationship developed between our school and Abbotsholme. At the time our school had been set up the Abbotsholme fees had been increased. This meant the Abbotsholme parents had a grudge against our school. I have no idea whether this increase in fees had been used to fund the launch of Doveleys, but the resentment bubbled away into open hostility.

One bright morning in the summer of 1953, just as breakfast had finished, an announcement was made that the Governors had decided to close Doveleys. All the boys would be moving to Abbotsholme to enlarge that school. It came as a devastating surprise to us boys, but had we been older we would have seen the writing on the wall. Some parents had complained that pupils sometimes did the washing up, a last ditch attempt to keep costs down. Since it is not possible to rerun life again I don't know if I would have achieved more at another school, but I have no regrets about going to Doveleys. No one would have persuaded me to send my own children to a boarding school though. At the end of term my parents came in their car and picked up all my belongings including the bantams. Watson came out and said 'Bye Simper, see you again.' But I never have. The world I had briefly belonged to, and all my friends, just vanished. I felt very alone.

Nearly fifty years later, after a Bawdsey Haven Yacht Club talk at Bawdsey Manor, a man I didn't recognize came up to me and said, 'Does the name Doveleys mean anything to you?'

I had always wondered if I would run into an ex-Doveleys boy one day, but was taken totally by surprise when it happened. I was even more surprised that the Derbyshire artist John Wilford remembered my dramatic shipwreck paintings that had been on the Art Room walls.

The next day we had a long talk and I discovered that Hugh Maw had become Headmaster of a Quaker School in southern England while some of Lewis Heath's art material was passed on to John after his death. I realized, although we had led very different working lives, how very similar we were in outlook. I decided to follow this up and try and see what had become of some of the other boys. It was Pete Barton who was able to fill me in with some of the details about what had happened to other boys. He lives in Macclesfield and he had met several of them. I recognized the names of my former school friends and there was a common factor. They seemed to have a total disinterest in anything competitive, but have a very great determination to pursue their own interests. I am unaware of anyone having reached great fame or wealth, but happy marriages and a fulfilled life seemed to be normal. This might be of some interest to educationists.

Chapter Two

Down on the River

Roughly speaking, during World War II, wherever you were in East Anglia you were never more than five miles away from a US Air Force base. There were young men in American uniforms in most of the towns and villages and many young women were bowled over by them. All three daughters of the Garrard family in Alderton eventually married Americans and went to live in California. Their father Jack Garrard was the butcher in the village. He had a paddock just up the road where he kept animals waiting to be slaughtered. Every Monday morning he drove two steers; two sheep and two pigs down the road and pole axed them in the shed at the back. It was very hard work butchering up these animals and in 1946 he decided to go to Los Angeles and live near his daughters.

The move proved to be a tough one because the high value of the dollar meant that he arrived in Los Angeles with much of his capital gone and he had to take quite menial jobs which was hard on a man approaching retirement age.

When Jack Garrard left he gave his open fishing boat *Lassie* to his son. The *Lassie* was kept on a mooring at Ramsholt Dock and, although only just over twenty years old, she had a strong desire to leak. When I left school it was suggested that, since I went trawling on the *Lassie*, I might like to 'keep an eye on her.'

I was off like a flash on my bike down to the river. I hauled the leaky dinghy *Dream,* that Jack Garrard had found drifting at sea, down the mud and rowed across to find the water over *Lassie's* floorboards. Looking back it seems to have been a prelude to a lifetime of pumping out wooden boats and pandering to their general needs.

After about four years John Garrard moved to Norfolk and took the *Lassie* with him. The last time I saw her she was a sad abandoned hulk in the corner of the docks at King's Lynn.

My father then decided he would like to have a boat. In 1951 we went up to Wroxham and had a trip down the Broads in the motor cruiser *Merry Princess.* This cruiser was purchased and Father's first move was to install a large drinks cabinet in the cabin. I was far more interested in the 12ft open clinker dinghy *Swallow,* which he had bought as a tender, and was delighted to learn that she had a red lugsail. The *Swallow* was chosen because she appeared to be very stable, but she was an awkward boat and was a pig to row any distance. Since it did not have a centreboard the dinghy didn't sail well either. On my first attempt at sailing I hoisted the sail upside down and started out from the shore without realizing my mistake. Luckily there was not enough wind to get me into any trouble as I hastily reset the sail. The learning process had begun.

The *Swallow's* most famous voyage came just after the 1953 Floods. During the night of the worst storm of the twentieth century a huge wall of water funnelled south down the North Sea, overriding the sea defences as it went. The really sad thing was that there was no warning system, while people were being drowned in their homes on the north Norfolk coast the tide moved on to cause further loss of life to the unsuspecting people further south.

In our village there was no loss of life, but there was complete devastation of the low-lying land. People woke to find that the sea had broken through every defence. Where there had been fields and grazing marshes, there was shiny silvery water. Father's chickens should have been pecking about on an open grass marsh, but instead they were sitting in their huts surrounded by water. To effect a rescue Father went down to Ramsholt Dock and set off in the *Swallow*. He had to row two miles down the river and then another mile over flooded marshes to retrieve the poor birds from their watery perches.

Floods and river defences seem to be very much part of coastal life. During World War II I went, with Father, to see some Italian prisoners of war repairing the river wall in front of Peyton Hall. The river wall was covered in men working by hand, filling up wheelbarrows and putting dirt on top of the wall. Repairs after the 1953 Floods were much more mechanized. The Woodbridge builders Ingram Smith got the contact to close one of the River Deben gaps. They had put a corrugated iron wall across the gap, rigged up a drag bucket on a wire rope and hauled mud up from the ooze to dump over the corrugated iron and recreate a new wall. They had almost closed the gap, when all the wet mud and corrugated iron collapsed sideways and they had to start all over again. The Flood was a catastrophic blow to the area, but once the gaps had been closed, it was amazing how quickly the whole tragedy was forgotten.

The gap Ingram-Smith's closed had been a dammed off creek mouth. Just down river from this was another creek with a low cottage beside it. I accompanied my father on a trip down to this gap and we were invited into The Cottage for a cup of tea. We sat on an old sofa in a timber-framed room with a low ceiling, and I had no idea that this would be The Cottage where I would live in the future. At the time we left up the muddy track full of potholes, and I thought no more about it.

Once I left school my thoughts and aims were mainly about pubs, sailing and girls. Quite soon I found I was going around with just one girl.

I would like to record that the first time I met Pearl was a life-defining moment. However I chiefly remember that Young Farmer's Club dance at Hadleigh because one young man had turned up in Wellington boots with the tops turned down, which was the fashion at the time. As Pearl worked in London I used to collect her from York House and go to parties in a friend's flat at Lennox Gardens. Once we went to a ball at the 'Dorchester', dress formal, no Wellingtons.

We agreed to get married but it was another two years before the wedding. When this event was being planned Pearl, always the practical one, said quite rightly, 'Where are we going to live?' A subject I had not thought much about. My first thoughts were to buy a sailing barge, live on it and take sailing holidays on it. Pearl said quietly, but firmly, that it was not a good idea to live on a boat of any sort. She wanted a home on dry land.

At this point we heard that The Cottage near The Creek with the plum trees in the garden was soon to become empty. It was a house near the water and filled both of our criteria. We were married in the summer of 1959 and returned from our honeymoon down the long lane to the lonely cottage. Following an old custom for good luck, I carried my new bride over the threshold. We had no idea that we would in fact be staying longer than anyone else had ever done in The Cottage in its four hundred years of existence.

An early autumn morning at The Cottage with Belle digging.

The Cottage, owned by an Estate, was being run on the lines of the Victorian feudal system, and unfortunately there was a reluctance to undertake repairs. Some cottages nearby were extremely basic, this did not seem to bother most people except when rain water came in. Our cottage had become the weekend retreat of a London family and was weather proof at least.

There were clearly many disadvantages to this rural home. Having the everlasting potholes in the long lane was a problem that has never gone away. The drinking water came from a well. In the early days I had to start the water pump every day, although sometimes I let it run too long and once the tank overflowed and water seeped into the bedroom. Fitting a ball cock solved the problem as it stopped the water from overflowing.

However oil lamps were a step too far back in time. We had a small generator installed, which ran some lights and just one electrical appliance. The generator worked well for a few years, but then the cut out switch gave problems. There we were living in this quiet, lonely spot with a huge diesel engine thumping away in the background. On a cold winter's night we would get into bed, switch off the last light and listen for the generator to stop. Often the generator didn't stop and I had to go out to the shed in the garden and switch it off.

The longer we stayed at The Cottage by The Creek, the harder it was to think of leaving. People kept knocking at the door and asking, sometimes demanding, to have the property 'when you leave.' It took a surprisingly long time before it dawned on me that I was in exactly the right place. On one side was the tidal river, since boats were the great passion of my life that was just right, and on the other side were fields in which I made a living.

Once, when I gave my address to a man in a builders merchant's in Woodbridge, he looked horrified and said with genuine pity, 'You don't live in that bloody awful place!'

He had grown up in The Cottage during the 1930s and his mother, 'her poor old feet were ever so bad', could not walk the four miles to Alderton or Shottisham. In the four years they lived there the mother of the family never left the cottage. In those days this was not unusual as there were shops in Woodbridge and Felixstowe that sent vans around to the remote groups of cottages with groceries, other household goods and clothes. When this family had moved to Woodbridge, a county town seven miles away, they had considered that they had arrived in the promised land. In the opinion of the man at the builder's merchant's The Cottage should have been pulled down long ago, no one should be expected to live in such an awful place without a road or street lights. This view of country living was shared by many people of his generation.

We had three great advantages over the other remote cottage dwellers. We had electricity, a car and a telephone, and these factors completely changed living in the country. We were in rural surroundings, but in direct contact with the outside world.

The phone was originally a shared line, not an ideal situation. At one stage the lady (well she was female anyway) on the party line used to pick up the phone and swear until I stopped talking. Fortunately this particular sharer of the party line moved off quite quickly. When living in a remote place you have a different set of problems to those in urban dwellings.

In retrospect, at least, many of the former occupants had fond memories of The Cottage and perhaps the most interesting of the former occupants had been Miss Butler. Her family had left in 1904 when she was eight and she did not return until she was eighty. She came walking down the lane with all the vigour of someone half her age. Once inside, memories of her Edwardian childhood came flooding back.

Miss Butler's father seems to have been a man of many skills. He had built a boat and worked as a forester. In a lean-to at the back of The Cottage there had been a blacksmith shop where farm horses had come to be shod. Butler had been one of a group of new people brought into the area by a new landowner at the end of the nineteenth century.

This London financier had built up an enormous fortune dealing in stocks and shares. He came down into East Suffolk and bought up most of five villages to create a sporting estate. However this had not been popular with the local establishment, they resented the rich Londoner coming in and building an ostentatious country house overlooking the sea. In the long run the villagers became very loyal to the new estate, but in the short term the estate owner had brought in newcomers. Mr Butler was one of these new recruits brought in to bring new life to the community and he asked for our cottage, which had been split into three, to be put into one.

One wild night the Butler's son, who had been visiting friends in Sutton, was cycling back along the river wall in the dark when there was a loud bang and he was thrown off his cycle. The river wall had burst open behind him. This was probably the 1904 flood when a tide went 6ft 3inches above the normal level. A barge alongside Ramsholt Dock had floated up on top of the quay, but fortunately they got her off on the next tide. It must have been this tide that broke through at the old creek mouth near our cottage and flooded inland for a mile to the gardens of Wood Hall. Butler and his wife heard the water roaring as it flooded the marshes and were very relieved when their son appeared at speed out of the darkness.

The new estate owner may have been incredibly wealthy, but you don't amass money by spending freely and he refused to pay for the river wall to be repaired, claiming that this was the River Board's responsibility. This is an argument that has been going on down the centuries; medieval records are full of squabbles over who paid for river defences.

Anyway for several years, in the Edwardian period, there was a wooden footbridge over the break in the river wall near The Cottage. The Cottage's only other land link to the outside world was a two-mile long rough farm track. In an age when most country people walked everywhere, living four miles from the nearest shop was a serious disadvantage.

The Butlers decided to leave and moved completely away from the Parish. They felt isolated and had been un-nerved by the 1904 flood. The new land magnate's aim to rebuild all the villages petered out quite quickly. After his death his son took over and concentrated mostly on pheasant shooting. However for a brief period, the village of Bawdsey was remodelled, some cottages were pulled down and new workers were brought in.

The Cottage always appears to have been part of a large estate, until we got the ownership, with the result that there is virtually no documentation relating to it. This makes dating the original building very difficult. Once a young man from English Heritage came and looked around the building and announced that the oldest part, a typical 'Suffolk longhouse', probably dated from about 1600. Sometime around 1800 another brick cottage was added on one end and it appears to have all been thatched until 1914.

For years I have tried to work out the location of the original stairs, there are no clues to them at all. It is just possible that this cottage, like many others, simply had a trap door and a ladder. It is most likely that the floors were originally dirt. At some later stage Our Cottage was given a brick herring-bone pattern floor in the middle room, well after it was built, and the other floors were probably cemented when the Butlers moved in.

Dirt floors lived on in Suffolk villages in quite large numbers until the 1960s. In some farmhouse kitchens they used to put straw on the floor to take the mud from the men's boots. In one cottage, just inland, which had a dirt floor, the practice had been to pull up the carpet every year and put another layer of newspapers on the floor. When the cottage was finally 'modernised', much to the disgust of the old lady living there, they found papers going back to 1856.

Although people living in the farms and cottages had very basic living standards, they were not actually much different to those in the poorer parts of Woodbridge. In this little market town the sewage ran straight out into the River Deben in the 1930s, but many houses still had a pail in the privy. In Angel Lane the people used to leave their doors unlocked at night so that 'Bargee' Gouch could walk through at night and empty the pails. 'Bargee' emptied this 'night soil' into the back of his little van and then took it down and tipped it into the river.

It was the poor rural housing conditions that caused 'the drift from the land', which took place in the decades either side of World War II. In the Sandlings area of East Suffolk the introduction of electricity, mains water and sewerage was much more difficult because houses were dotted around the landscape. There were few real village centres before the planners starting putting houses in groups.

Our Parish was typical of the scattered villages on the edge of the great open Sandlings sheep walks. In 1859 203 people had lived here, but in 2004 only 25 people lived in the Parish. There had been plenty of work on the farms and in the coprolite pits. There are traces of eleven pits in the parish and in about 1860, at the height of the boom, the landlords did very well out of it. Coprolite, the fossilized remains of pre-historic animal dung, was dug out by hand and taken around to Ipswich by barge for crushing into super phosphate of lime. Our parish was then part of the Waller estate, based on Wood Hall in the next village and they put up the money to build the parish school in 1879.

The coprolite pits closed when cheaper phosphates began to be shipped in from Chile. Cheap food was also flooding in from North America and the new British Empire countries and this killed the agricultural economy. There was simply not enough work for all the people living in The Parish and they moved away. The shop closed in the 1880s, the school closed in 1928.

The only work in the Parish was on the farms, but machines were steadily replacing people. In the 1930s an elderly couple had lived in our cottage, he was a cowman at the Lodge Farm. A boating man once told me that before the War it had been the custom for people to row or sail down from Woodbridge and ask the woman at The Cottage for a glass of water, in exchange for a small coin. The water was said to hold special properties, perhaps an ancient holy well. In 1940 there was a very hard winter and with wartime fuel shortages Dr Lund stated that as he couldn't get down to them the elderly couple should be moved to a village. When the boating people returned after World War II The Cottage garden had grown up with brambles, and because the place was empty people went in and helped themselves to the little yellow plums in the garden.

During the hard winter of 1940 the Lowestoft trawling smack *Colinda* broke loose from her moorings at Waldringfield and was sunk, by the ice, opposite The Creek. The smack had been one of the last to fish out of Lowestoft under sail, but had been bought by an RAF pilot stationed at Martlesham Heath. He had sailed her back to Waldringfield single handed and lived aboard her, but sadly he was killed in the Battle of Britain. Bert Scopes told me that her mast had stuck up out of the river all through the War and eventually Trinity House came and blew her up. People used to get their trawls caught on her iron-work and over the years odd bits of the smack have been washed ashore.

In about 1947 The Cottage got its second reprieve. It was repaired and slightly updated because a member of the Estate owner's family wanted to use it as a holiday retreat. To do this refurbishment the estate workers used recycled material from other more prestigious properties.

I remember the craftsmen of the Old Estate. Every morning this band of elderly men met at the Estate Yard and a rather ancient lorry would transport them to the property that was under repair at the time. Nothing was ever done too quickly. Many of them held extreme socialist views, and I remember one of them talking about the 'sharing out of wealth' in terms which suggested that he was a supporter of communism. When the Old Estate, forced by taxation, sold much of its property the family were greatly concerned that all the 'loyal workers' should buy their homes at a nominal sum.

In about 1954 the Estate Agent was a bit surprised when one of the former farm bailiffs turned up and demanded to buy his house. He had a bag of cash with him, which included gold sovereigns. He had always had a lucrative sideline in selling the Old Estate's milk and other goods he regarded as 'surplus'. It was said in the village that so long as a man touched his hat to the titled owner of the Estate he could do as he pleased.

Perhaps the most significant post-war change to The Cottage was the laying down of a lawn and some flowerbeds. The garden had been a purely practical place to provide food for the working country people living there. It took on the new role of giving pleasure to a London-based family enjoying the open-air life in the summer and was the forerunner of this type of cottage.

There was still a vegetable patch when we came to live at The Cottage in 1959. There is enormous satisfaction to be had from growing your own vegetables, but sadly digging, and a bad back, just didn't mix so this was soon dropped. To my surprise I found I could write a book during the winter and spring, the same amount of work as it took to prepare the vegetable garden for another season, and a book reaped more reward than the cost of a few vegetables.

My answer to gardening was a larger lawn, but it meant hours and hours of walking up and down behind a tiny lawn mower in the summer. If I could re-live my life again the one thing I would do, above all others, is to buy a 'ride on' mower far earlier.

After our three children, Caroline, Joanna and Jonathan, had left home Pearl's interest in flowers came to the surface. The joint approach to gardening was not pretentious patches of totally alien plants imposed in the Suffolk countryside, but to make the garden simply a part of surrounding countryside. Buttercups and daisies are seen as a colourful addition to the lawn.

The 'blending in' approach included having minimal garden fences, which did not work. One of the many incidents I remember is suddenly seeing an elderly couple smashing down our hedge to get into the garden. They were not at all apologetic and said they were 'taking the short cut'. It turned out that they had misread their Ordnance Survey map and were in the wrong place. We put up a high fence and, after a party of walkers stopped and had a picnic on the back lawn, a gate. It is not that there is a shortage of footpaths, it is just that some 'trail blazers' seem to see the countryside as a challenge. Fortunately most of the increasing numbers of people who visit the countryside manage to do it with limited disturbance to the wildlife or rural residents.

By living in a remote place one is constantly surprised by the unlikely things that happen in the countryside. Once I discovered a man lying in his car outside The Cottage. Shortly before this my brother-in-law had discovered a suicide on his farm and I was a bit concerned about this chap. It turned out that he was asleep; that was a relief. He was from the University of Wales at Swansea and had driven overnight just to visit our creek as part of some research. He had a copy of Jeffrey's 'British Conchology', a Victorian textbook published in 1869, which recorded that our creek had its own species of winkle. It even had its own Latin name, *Littorina obtusata* var *aestuaii*, and disclosed that the original specimens collected by Jeffreys were in the US National Museum in Washington. This was all rather exciting news. However our visitor, who turned out to be Dr Brian James, said that it was highly unlikely that such a species existed and that he wished to prove this was a Victorian collector's error.

We asked him in for breakfast and he clearly enjoyed my mother-in-law's blackberry jelly. After that, he started a thorough search of The Creek, but he did not find the rare winkle. Then I realised that Jeffreys must have been writing about the old Victorian creek mouth, which had silted up after the sluice was moved. In the eighteenth century there had been an oyster fishery in this reach and the ownership of the foreshore went with it. Our researcher continued his hunt in the Old Creek and to his considerable surprise found the exact winkles. Months later we received a letter to say that it was not a separate species, but a form of the flat periwinkle that grows in brackish water.

At other times we have had ambulances arrive because walkers have been in trouble. One man was dead on arrival at hospital, another was carried away with a broken leg and we never heard what happened to him. Walking with our dog Belle one evening I saw a man collapsed on the ground and moved towards him. I thought 'another heart attack, act quickly,' then I saw two up turned ladies feet under him! I quietly called Belle over to the other side of the river wall thinking that at that hopefully magic moment, they would not have welcomed a wet inquisitive Labrador's nose.

At least Belle is friendly to passing walkers, our first dog, Tibsy, hated them. The legendary Tibsy was bought from the Hunt Kennels at Hadleigh. A fine strong fox terrier with an overriding instinct to kill foxes, but at that stage foxes had not returned to The Parish, so he went for walkers instead. We would see Tibsy roaring out of the garden, defending his territory, and then cries of pain, and sometimes the most appalling swearing, when he chased a passing walker away.

The Estate changed hands shortly after we went to live in the Cottage and the new owners were thrilled when the Duke of Edinburgh attended their large-scale pheasant shoots. Tibsy went off and joined one of these shoots, he loved hunting pheasants, but the keepers probably did not need an uncontrolled dog making the birds break cover at the wrong moment. I am quite certain if 'the Guns' had not been in sight the keepers would happily have shot the troublesome dog. I spent the most embarrassing day of my life, keeping out of sight, looking for the wretched dog. It was later reported to me that he had joined the royal personage for some time, but because he was enjoying himself, behaved perfectly. He was less well mannered with a minor royal figure.

Even when the pheasant-shooting season finished at the end of January the New Estate owners wanted to continue shooting so they went after wildfowl. The Old Estate had created the first of several 'flight ponds' on the marshes. Flight ponds are either 'morning' or 'evenings' ponds depending on how the duck fly in to rest from feeding on the tideway. Once in 1964 they decided to have an evening flight shoot, someone had the bright idea of sending a royal gun wildflowling at dusk on the river wall in front of our cottage. Unfortunately no one explained this to our watchful little terrier.

Anyway Tibsy suddenly got the scent of a stranger lurking about in the dusk at the bottom of the garden. The small terrier was off 'like a shot out of a gun' to defend his territory. To find out what was happening I followed at speed. What I saw was a figure, which I was later told was one William of Gloucester, running along the river wall hotly pursued by a small, determined terrier. I am happy to report that on this occasion no royal blood was drawn, but a smart pair of plus fours may well have needed some stitching.

The neighbours in The Creek

My rather bad-tempered fox terrier was of great concern to my family when they had their own children. Since the grandchildren spent a lot of time with us it was suggested that I had a Labrador. When Jonathan's wife's Labrador produced a litter I was offered the first pick. I chose Belle, a calm female and the smallest of the litter (the nearest one to a terrier?) It was love at first sight.

Dogs, of all domestic animals, appear to actually enjoy the company of human beings. However the practice of 'taking the dog for a walk' is really designed for humans. Most dogs, given the chance, will happily run off by themselves.

In the early 1980s, when marsh harriers had recently returned to the Sandlings coast, Pearl and I took the dog for a walk up the Marsh Valley. High above the reed beds a marsh harrier was silently hovering in the sky. We were on the way to see Ronny Chapman who was digging 'grups', small gullies to let the surface water run into the ditch. Ronny was one of the old school of true countrymen and as he had been on his own all day, was very keen to have a chat.

'I've been thinking,' said Ronny, his bright red face up turned under his cloth cap, 'I have spent my whole working life on the land within sight of these marshes. I started with Miller at Pettistree Hall as a horseman'. He pointed towards a farm we both knew lay beyond the fir trees on Sutton Knoll. Then he used his shovel to point up the valley, 'After that I worked for Victor Shepherd at Shottisham Hall, he was a rum old boy' Ronny laughed with affection, 'then I come here. That's funny to think about that stood here, it's all gone very quickly'.

Ronny was a bachelor, but typical of the old farm workers who lived and worked all their lives within a few minutes cycle ride from their homes. A few years later he gave up full time farm work and in the winter went beating at the New Estate's pheasant shoots. Once he failed to turn up and a mate went around to his cottage and found him dead on the floor.

I now know how Ronny had felt, time does go very quickly, but it is difficult to measure passing time in the country. In a town each street belongs to a particular period of history. People writing books point to the architectural merits of certain streets, highlighting the period they belong to. You don't get that in the countryside. The fields and woods seem timeless, nature is renewing itself all the time, trees fall and new ones appear, but you can't put a date to anything. Ronny has been gone well over twenty years, but the reeds and ditches in the Marsh Valley remain very much the same and marsh harriers still hunt over them.

A winter family walk, 1994. Simon, Matthew, Clare, Caroline, Laura, Tom & Joanna.

Chapter Three

Wild Weather

Look around any waterside place in eastern England and you will often find marks carved on walls, usually with a date beside them. These will be a record of some great flood of the past. At Twickenham, on the wall opposite Eel Pie Island, '1774' is carved, remembering the March flood of that year when heavy rain put the fresh water up 8ft over its normal level, causing chaos all along the river and sweeping away Henley Bridge. At Southwold down on the harbour there is a mark and '1953' on the front of the 'Sole Bay Inn.' Coastal people measure time in floods and great gales; they are the important events in life.

Floods are terrible, but there are few traces of them within a few years. This is an ongoing problem. The Anglo-Saxon Chronicles record that in about 1020 the great landowners, whose cattle and land were being destroyed by the sea, went to King Canute and begged for help. Canute, son of a Viking, was one of the most powerful kings in Western Europe. Canute was a man who made things happen, but he was also a pragmatic man. He went down to the seashore and commanded the tide not to come in. Canute was very aware the tide would come in, but he then turned to his followers and said, in effect, ' I can't do anything about it, so don't bother me on this subject again.' This seems to have been the policy of central government ever since. Instead of ordering the tides back masses of reports are made.

One can't blame Canute; he had no method of fighting the formidable power of the North Sea. The offshore drilling industry has brought to light the fact that waves in the North Sea are far larger than anyone realised. An extreme storm can produce 100ft waves and even in the southern North Sea, drilling rigs have been hit by 60ft waves. As these huge walls of water thunder in toward the coast the offshore sandbanks break their force. In theory banks and shallow water break the force of seas and reduce them so that only 25ft waves actually reach the coast. If the offshore banks go, by dredging or erosion, the whole of East Anglia has no protection from the force of the North Sea.

The power of the sea and tide is so tremendous that their combined forces can cause terrible destruction. Even the rocky coasts of western Britain are very slowly being eroded by the Atlantic storms so that it is not surprising that the soft sand coast of East Anglia, which has about as much natural resistance to the force of the waves as wet cardboard, is being swept into the sea. Once land has gone into the sea it is never replaced, and on a small island with a large population it is a very serious problem.

On the estuaries changes happen much more slowly, but they happen all the same. In the early 1970s I realised that the saltings at the entrance of The Creek were starting to crumble down on to the ooze mud. At the time no one was much interested in these

Yachts washed ashore at Ramsholt the morning after the 1987 Hurricane.

Erosion of the saltings in the same place as the Hurricane photograph, 16 years later.

changes to the estuaries, apart from lone wildfowlers most people kept away from the mud around the rivers.

About that time the sluice in the creek down river from ours kept silting up and was causing difficulties because it was the only way to drain some grazing marshes. The Manager in charge of the repair gang invited the agent for The Estate and myself to come and see the problem they were having on the ooze with the sluice channel.

'Follow me' he instructed, 'and I will show you what we are up against.'

We followed him as he marched boldly out on to the soft-silt mud. Just before we reached the edge of the river the agent, a robust rugby-playing sort of chap, got stuck. The more he struggled the deeper his boots went down into the mud.

I tried to pull the agent out, but felt I was also going in and suggested to the Manager that his gang, who were all standing watching on the river wall, might come and help.

'Oh,' he replied, in triumph, 'that is the point I am making. They have refused to come out here!'

The agent was not pleased about this dangerous way of making a point, but he behaved with great courage when we left him alone out on the ooze. He was convinced that the tide was coming in, actually it was the last of the ebb. As we left him he suggested we went to the pub and called for a helicopter. I was then about thirty and at the peak of my mud walking performance, but it had still been a struggle to reach the saltings. However once back the gang was persuaded into collecting some branches off the trees and we made a path out to the trapped agent.

The agent had been totally stuck in the mud and unable to free himself, but eventually he made it back to dry land and left, covered in mud, minus his boots. This had been a very anxious time for all of us. The conclusion of this meeting was that a new sluice channel was dug elsewhere. As the years have passed that sluice has also silted up.

A few years before this mud incident there had been an almost fatal case of a US Air Force pilot who had been forced to bail out and had come down on the soft ooze off Iken Church. The force of the impact meant that he had sunk in right up to his neck. I can't think of a worse situation to be in. The only thing he could do was shout. Fortunately it was a still calm winter's afternoon and the men working on the farm nearby heard him. They got ladders and planks and rescued him.

Since the 1970s the rate of erosion of the saltings in the estuaries has speeded up and the top of the ooze mud has started to be whipped away in places. River channels and offshore banks have always moved, but in the second half of the twentieth century all the estuaries on the East Coast started to have the same problems with channels expanding, and with creeks and wharves silting up.

In 1900 there were farm wharves in most creeks and barges went in to load. Many creeks can only be entered with a dinghy now. Presumably the increased flow of tidal water washing away the banks has created silt that settles where there is still water.

When we went to live in The Cottage in 1959 I used to row across the river at low tide and collect winkles from a large spit. Yachts were constantly going ashore on this spit and further up river they also went aground on the Middle Ground, another mud bank. Both of these underwater banks have been completely washed away. With the saltings eroding back and the ooze level dropping, the river is like a great lion shaking off its chains and breaking free to take the land at its will.

The river wall on Hemley Point where the tide broke through in the 1930s. When I first saw it in 1950 there was a small gap in the wall, but by 2004 most of the wall had been washed away and there was a huge gap.

A contributing factor to the erosion in the estuaries has been the loss of eel grass. This long weed slowed down the flow of the tide over the ooze. It was also the preferred home of eels and the food for Brent geese. A hard frost in 1881 resulted in the ice tearing up the eel grass by the roots from off Mersea Island and it did not return. There was eel grass right up the River Deben until the 1930s when the newly tarred roads were blamed for its disappearance. In theory the sea level has been rising by about 2mm a year. However the actual tides do not seem to be higher than they were fifty years ago. This theoretical measurement appears to have been arrived at because there are more high tides, which means more water going in and out of the estuaries. However the researches of Dr Rob Hughes have shown that increasingly ragworm are eating more vegetation on the saltings, making them crumble at the edges. The increasing estuary erosion might not be the result of a tidal lion created by Global Warming, but simply millions of hungry ragworms.

On the coast long sloping shingle beaches are needed to break the force of the waves rolling in. In the past the vast quantity of shingle and sand on the coast was seen as a natural resource to be quarried. In the nineteenth century barges, and before them schooners, going north for coal would go on to Landguard Point, Bawdsey Ferry and Shingle Street to collect shingle. This shingle was sold for dock construction in the north of England. On the Essex coast the story was much the same, shingle moved south to Colne Point where it was loaded into barges for glass making, while off Shoebury Ness the sand went for brick making.

The shifting shingle knolls at the entrance of the River Deben in March, 2003.

Frank Knights, who grew up in Melton, remembers there were often three or four barges lying with road making material at the Suffolk County Council wharf at Wilford Bridge. When the Woodbridge by-pass was built in the 1930s thousands of tons of shingle were brought up river by barge from the knolls on the Deben Bar. This was a regular, but very low return, trade. Captain Skinner had two barges that dropped alongside the knolls at the Deben Bar, to shovel shingle down a chute into the hold and take it up river. Frank remembers following George Skinner from Kyson Point as he 'turned' the 73ft barge *Tuesday* against the wind all the way up to Wilford Bridge. Captain Skinner died in 1935 and Ted Marsh, the river pilot, continued, with a steel ship's lifeboat *Iron Duke,* working shingle up to the Ferry Dock.

A more ambitions venture was started at Sun Wharf with the 88ft motor barge *Justice,* a former wooden boomie barge. She was fitted with a suction dredge and loaded 140 tons. Harold Paice, who worked on the *Justice* for about three years, remembered that they did up to three trips a week, but sometimes they worked off Harwich and took shingle up to Parkeston Quay.

During World War II a larger quantity of shingle was taken to build the airfields. Bentwaters' first runway was built with 800 tons of shingle from Kessingland. Shingle from Shingle Street was taken to make the runways for Debach airfield, but this had not been a great success because there was so much driftwood in the shingle that the first runway broke up. Numerous wrecks are buried in the shingle around Orfordness. In about

The *Three Sisters* crossing the Deben bar on a calm day. In an onshore wind the breaking seas make the entrance very dangerous.

1952 the shingle in front of Shingle Street eroded exposing the timbers of a wooden ship wrecked in the 1890s at the river entrance in front of the Martello Tower. This was the *Rudolf,* a Rye built schooner that had traded to Orford with coal. The pilots bringing her in had lost control of her and the force of the tide sweeping her into the beach burst the bow open.

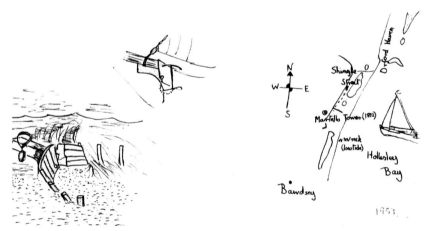

After World War II it was realised that the shingle was part of the natural defences and beach quarrying was stopped. Attention then switched to serious offshore dredging to fulfil the construction industry's insatiable demand for aggregate. Frankly it seemed a better idea to dig holes in the seabed rather than turn the English countryside into a series of quarries. Attention shifted to dredging further off the coast and a major industry sprung up around the coast of South East England bringing in countless millions of tonnes of aggregate. It is a real dilemma, the construction industry needs aggregate, but what long-term effect does it have on coastal erosion?

The East Lane, Bawdsey in 2004. Rocks were protecting the beach, but within two years the sea was eating its way around them.

The whole business of coastal drift is highly complex, dredging in Harwich Harbour to deepen the channel appears to have resulted in more silt being carried out to sea and the Cork Sands have grown. There are problems with erosion when the material that should replenish beaches and offshore banks is taken away. It may be a coincidence, but on the East Coast of England where there is offshore dredging bad erosion appears on the corresponding coast. In The Netherlands offshore dredging was abandoned because of its effect on the coast.

Some people, particularly those who have moved into the area, seem to see nothing wrong with coastal villages and towns going into the sea. At Southwold they even fought to stop coastal defences!

On either side of Southwold the sea is eating away the land, particularly just to the north at Easton Bavents where Peter Boggis lives. In order to safeguard his home Peter Boggis brought in thousands of tonnes of soil, at his own expense, and put it on the cliff face. Was anyone pleased? The town rose in protest and the council stopped him, 'to consider the environmental impact.' The environmental impact must be that, if that piece of coast is not protected, the sea will go behind Southwold, in the fullness of time, and the whole place will become another victim of 'badly managed retreat'. With the sea, doing nothing has never proved to be the best option.

The official line has always been that defence against land going into the sea was too expensive, but it is more complex than that. Dunwich Parish Meeting wanted to adopt a natural barrier of marram grass and high-density mesh to hold the foreshore against the impact of major storms. This low-key traditional form of defences was infinitely less expensive than major projects that the Environment Agency seem to be geared up to sponsor.

Peter Boggis on the cliffs he was defending at Eastern Bavents, 2003. Most of the headland that had once been the most easterly point in England is now under the sea.

In truth Dunwich, with the shallow sea in front of the crumbling cliffs, seems to be a good candidate to have the offshore reefs that have been successful at Sea Palling and Jaywick. The Environment Agency seem to have found it easier to obtain finance for major projects, that take many years in preparation, and have objected to a low key attempt at Dunwich. Poor Dunwich, we have learnt nothing after centuries of destruction.

The sailing barge *Marjorie* off the crumbling cliffs of Walton Naze, 2001. In 2004 Michelle Nye-Browne opened the Tower as a visitors centre.

At Walton Naze, the Tower was built in 1720 as a navigational aid and the land seems to have been receding at an average rate of 3m a year. Attempts to increase sea defences were frustrated for a while by English Nature because they claimed that it would damage the cliffs! It is a curious twist of fate that an organization set up to safeguard the environment actually seems to be frustrating sea and river defences. Sometimes the sea is only part of the problem.

If the Government's predicted rise in sea level actually takes place, Britain is in real trouble. The Government believe that this country has more land below sea level than The Netherlands. The problem is a great deal more serious than just a few coastal bungalows slipping into the North Sea, it will affect everyone living in the British Isles, one way or another. The coast is highly fragile, if an area is allowed to flood then the whole coastline can become unstable and simply wash away. Most of the coastal counties are at risk and vast areas could go into the sea. We could end up living in high rise flats in the Midlands!

Coastal erosion, the cancer of the coast, is such a serious subject that most people prefer not to think about it, but they do care passionately about the coast. In 2003 a torrent of passion was released when a Scallop sculpture was put on the open beach between Aldeburgh and Thorpeness. Originally the Scallop sculpture had been destined to go in Aldeburgh, but the town wouldn't have it. So as a compromise it was sited on the open beach. Some liked it and others absolutely demanded that it was removed as quickly as possible. Art released a response that a North Sea storm failed to do. If only people could devote the same enthusiasm to demanding coastal defences.

For many years after the 1953 Floods warnings of high tides were taken very seriously, we got regular warnings about abnormally high tides and have gradually taken them less seriously. One calm winter evening in the 1960s we got a Flood Warning, it was snug and warm in the living room and I didn't really want to go outside, but went begrudgingly. It was a lovely moonlit night and I walked down to the river wall where to my horror I found the River Deben had become an inland sea.

The river was considerably higher than a good spring tide. Instead of the waves breaking on the saltings, they were coming all the way down from Woodbridge and throwing driftwood on to the top of the river wall.

There in the moonlight I could see that my 28ft *Sea Fever* had pulled up all her winter berth anchors and she was banging up against the river wall. Left there she would have been high and dry until the next summer.

Pearl and I dragged the pram dinghy a hundred yards down from the top garage and spent ages rowing around picking up the anchors and relaying them. It was a race against time and the tide was already falling when we finally hauled *Sea Fever* back into her proper berth. We returned to the warmth of the living room, wet and tired, and The Cottage seemed so safe after the turmoil of the open river at the bottom of the garden.

The following winter she broke loose again, I returned from work to find *Sea Fever's* bow on the edge of the laying-up creek and the hull laying over at a great angle. We returned at the next high tide, not quite as high as the previous one, and managed to lever the bow up so that she slipped back into the water. After that I took the 'winter berth' much more seriously, holding the anchors in with posts and putting old mooring chain on the mooring ropes so that the weight held her in place.

A rain shower over The Creek.

When we laid the 35ft *L'Atalanta* up in The Creek it was a major operation involving a network of rope and chain. Once this heavy 35ft Swedish customs cutter managed to break away from her mooring on an autumn high tide and gale and went up on the foreshore. She stayed there all winter and I kept hoping that there would be a tide high enough to float her off. We had to wait until the following spring and then Frank Knights and Geoffrey Ingram-Smith came down river and towed us off. Boats, like children, can get up to an awful a lot of mischief if left on their own for too long.

The winter *L'Atalanta* lay on the foreshore was quite a mild one, just a few days of freezing weather when the ice came drifting down from the freshwater Deben. The winter 1962-63 was the worst we have experienced. It started the weekend before Christmas when the ground froze hard, the frost sunk deeper into the ground so that by the middle of February it was like concrete. The first batch of heavy snow came on New Year's Eve when we were at a party at the 'White Lion', Aldeburgh. We came outside to discover a thick white carpet of snow on the ground. It was freezing hard, but little wind. The first part of the journey home was on the main roads, which had been kept open by traffic, but after Melton we turned for the road to the Sandlings peninsula and found ourselves confronted, in the moonlight, with a desert of pure white drifting snow.

Military engineers had straightened out the roads across the Suffolk heaths during the Napoleonic War. The idea was that if the French army landed, the soldiers from the Garrison at Woodbridge could be marched quickly to repel the attack. The two miles of road across Sutton Walks, apart from one bend in the middle, is straight. Before the trees were planted the heath was completely open. The first part of Sutton Walks was downhill so that we crushed slowly through the snow. Then we reached Saxon's Bottom, the valley in the middle of heath, and started to go uphill. The wheels spun at once and we were stuck for the first time.

According to local legend the Saxons and Danes fought a great battle in the Bottom. It would have been a good time to have seen some ghostly armies locked in terrible combat, but we were totally alone in the open, completely silent countryside.

Luckily we had taken a shovel and a length of old stair carpet for such an emergency. I dug out the snow from under the back wheels and put the carpet under them. Pearl drove forward until we got stuck again. It was well below freezing, but in spite of the cold I was sweating. Normally we had whistled up that hill in a few seconds, but we were over an hour fighting our way up the modest slope that time.

In January the snow increased and it got colder. When the wind got up we were soon snowed in. Snowploughs cleared the main rural roads, but we were two miles down a by-road and track and this was largely left alone. We were cut off from the rest of the world by the snow for three weeks.

One afternoon, January 19, I walked along beside the river and found it completely frozen over. Because the river is tidal the ice floes were moving and it would not have been safe to walk on. Up river, where it was narrower, a few daring people walked across the river on the ice at Woodbridge and Waldringfield, while in Martlesham Creek a football match was played on solid ice. I stood in the Cliff Wood looking down at the lower end of the Rocks Reach and wondered whether to waste a photograph on this iced up tidal river. I thought this might be a waste of film because I imagined that this type of weather happened quite often. In the forty-one winters since then there has never been that amount of ice again.

There is generally a hard winter every decade and they always start very quickly. Often we wake up to find the lane full of snow and The Cottage cut off from the nearby villages. When I had been at school in Staffordshire, snow had frequently been thick and most of the schoolboys had gone off tobogganing on a hill beside the River Dove. It had been tremendous fun, whistling down the hill and then fighting to stop before going into the river. The more daring boys went as far as they could and had to leap off before their sledges went over the high bank into the river. Although I would have liked my children to enjoy these thrills this proved impossible in our area. With limited snow the wind just blows it off making drifts in the nearest hedge. However when the children were young this didn't stop us from trying to find a good sledge run when we were snowed in.

We started off on the river wall, but that was a bit tame, so we set off to find a hill. We walk along with snow crunching under our feet and the three children squabbling over whose turn it was to tow the sledge. Near the church is a field called Broom Hill, which might have been promising, but there was hardly enough slope to get the sledge moving, let alone gain speed. As dusk approached we set off to walk home. In the sharp cold air, the only sounds were cock pheasants calling out to mark their territory. The lesson learnt from this excursion was not to try and fight our way out, but just enjoy the situation around us.

However it is sensible to try and keep open lines of communication with the outside world. Once in a wild winter gale the trees started to come down on The Parish loop road, our only way out, which resulted in a highly authorative phone call from the police demanding that we removed the trees from the road 'because it could save lives if an ambulance had to be sent in'. To clear the road Jonathan started work with a chainsaw at Peyton Hall corner while I threw the loose wood into the hedge. The wind howled in the trees above and made so much noise that we could hear nothing. To contact each other we had to get really close and shout. Then in a huge gust, which was almost impossible to stand against, a massive branch came crashing down between us. We began to think that we were only keeping the road open so that an ambulance would be able to reach us when we were crushed.

To survive in adverse weather we have learnt to develop our own form of self-sufficiency. By Christmas time we have oil for the lamps ready for the time when the freezing fog brings down the electric wires, and Pearl has a cupboard full of tinned food. We also build up a supply of firewood. When wooden boat building was a major industry at Woodbridge they helped to keep our home fires going through much of the winter. The spare off cuts either floated off the yards on a high tide or were just thrown in at the end of the day and came down river to us.

In the 1980s we let our grazing marshes to Chris Twinch and he revived the practice of grazing the saltings. This had been done before World War I as a cure for foot and mouth disease and they also put ewes on the saltings before they went to the tup, for the salt to increase their fertility. In the 1930's some animals with the foot and mouth disease were hidden, out of sight, so I was told, on lonely marshes where nobody went. By all accounts the cattle recovered from the disease.

In 1987 Chris' sheep were grazing on sugar beet tops on the high ground when there was another period of snow. With the roads closed he could not get down from his farm near Saxmundham. We thought we had better go and look at his flocks. One bunch on Bull Meadow had walked over the hedge on a snowdrift, but another bunch had vanished completely. They had been grazing on sugar beet tops on the Foxburrows, an exposed field open to the blasting north wind. Then we spotted four sheep's heads sticking out of a snowdrift. When we started to dig them out we realised that the rest of the bunch were also buried under snow. They had gathered down wind in the corner of the field and stayed there as the snow just piled up around them. Once released they happily bounded off across the field like spring lambs, frozen snow still clinging to their fleeces.

In the late afternoon, because our fresh food was in short supply, Jonathan and I set out in a tractor for the shop in Alderton. This was only about four miles away, but as we had to skirt around snowdrifts it took far longer than normal. The light was fading and it was snowing again by the time we arrived at Alderton Knoll. Ahead through the murky dusk we saw the lights of the shop in amongst the houses. After the wild waste of snow-covered fields it was like reaching the safety of civilisation.

Chapter Four

Living with the Neighbours

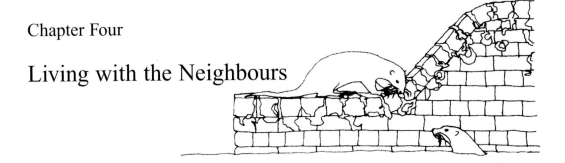

Every Christmas, amongst the cards from friends, we receive photographs of a snowy winter scene. If you enquire, it will turn out that these were never taken at Christmas, but some time in the New Year. I don't know why we make such a big deal in England of the possibility of a White Christmas. I have spent every Christmas of my life in Suffolk and have never seen a White Christmas. Frankly I don't expect to see one now and the whole myth of the Xmas countryside covered with snow is a piece of folklore dating back to some distant time of hard winters. One thing I do know is that the old pagans who started this mid-winter festivity got the date exactly right. There are bad gales to go with the autumn high tides, followed by fairly peaceful weather until Christmas. Then it suddenly gets colder and in the New Year the real winter arrives. I used to find January and February very difficult on the farm, every time I walked outside a cold wind went right through me. In March, with the East winds coming in from the North Sea it was still cold, but the days were getting longer and everything started to grow so that it was more cheerful. It is the most wonderful thing in the world to watch the crops you have planted suddenly start to grow. Every year the brown fields turned into green carpets of barley, often overnight.

The long cold winters hit our neighbours, the wading birds and wildfowl of the River Deben, very hard indeed. Theirs is a very fragile existence. Once, in the mid-1980s, we had only four days of freezing cold weather, but it killed hundreds of small birds. Walking along the tide line after the big freeze was pathetic, the tide had washed up a line of little feathered bodies. One had a job to miss them. The problem was that although the freeze had only lasted a few days, the ooze mud had frozen, thus cutting off their vital food supply. The falling temperatures did the rest.

Last winter we had a week of hard weather in January, but temperatures did not fall all that low. We could see the waders feeding out on the mud. All seemed well, but there was one near victim.

Our Labrador, Belle, started barking as soon as it got light. We thought the deer had got into the garden again. She hates them and goes wild at the mere glimpse of these majestic animals. I peered out of the window, expecting to see brown forms vanishing through the hedge. Instead I was looking at a very angry cob swan.

The swan was sitting on our lawn in a very bad temper. Clearly the poor bird was exhausted, his food supply must have been cut off by the bad weather. The swans mostly live up river, near Woodbridge, where there is plenty of fresh water coming down from the upper Deben. The fresh water freezes easily and becomes sheets of ice, but down where we are the salt water normally just freezes at the very edges. Nevertheless it had been really bad news for this old cob.

The swan during his winter visit to our garden.

Rushing indoors I got some bread, Pearl sympathised with my hasty action, but suggested porridge oats might be just as welcome to the swan. At that point in the weekly shopping cycle the bread had mostly gone, but there was still a packet of porridge oats in the cupboard. It did not matter, the cob was not interested in our offering, but he hissed vigorously when some ponies in the little meadow started reaching through to get the bread that he had left.

For a few days the cob became one of the family, moving around the garden searching for the best grass to eat. This totally wild bird did not seem to be at all bothered about us so long as we kept about ten feet away from him. I suppose since he and his mate (where was she?) had spend much of the summer hanging around anchored yachts, hissing for free food hand outs, they looked on humans as being a possible food supply. When the weather suddenly became warmer, he left.

Birds may nest in hedgerows but they also find food in the fields. Oil seed rape, although we never grew a lot of it, was particularly useful to provide food in the early summer. In May the bees found rape a good source of nectar, and the grain that had fallen on the ground at harvest time kept many birds alive right through the winter.

The pheasant was the wildlife species that affected our life the most. In fact most of our parish was remodelled to suit the habits of the proud and beautiful cock pheasants. Woods and belts had been planted to allow these birds to fly high over the waiting guns. Because of its sporting associations bird watchers take little notice of the pheasant, or for that matter, the smaller partridges, but they are most handsome birds.

From a nursery in Bawdsey young trees were taken out and planted to create woods and belts for pheasant cover. Our Parish, because it had a low population and wide-open fields, became a prime area for planting. Most of these trees had just reached maturity when the 1987 hurricane swept through and levelled most of them to the ground. The New Estate, who took over in 1959, also focused on shooting, although economics has forced them towards 'paid shoots.' To cater for demand they have moved toward partridge shooting, which does not require woods, just high fences to make 'the birds' fly higher. Even after a century of shooting the remodelling continued, and several areas of trees were grubbed out in an effort to get the pheasants to fly in the required direction.

Pheasants stay in the Parish so long as the gamekeepers provide food for them in the woods, however the seals in the river have to locate their own food supply. The seals are seen in the river in August, presumably they come for the mullet and seabass and stay the winter for the herring. The old fisherman used to say that a seal eats its own weight in fish every day. Several old-time fishermen carried rifles and used to shoot seals to prevent them from decimating fish stocks and damaging their nets.

Some of the Walton Backwaters seals in Oakley Creek. Great Oakley Dock, at the head of the creek where the explosive ships loaded, is one of the last of the creek wharves in use.

It was in 1962 that we saw a seal in The Creek. When the first seal appeared my original plan, coming from a rural background, was to turn it into a rug. I crept down to the river wall with a rifle, where the seal sat watching me with interest. I looked down the rifle sights into his eyes, then realised I could not possibly pull the trigger.

Since then, only one seal has appeared in the creek. Belle spotted it first, a white seal pup was asleep on the edge of the mud. The dog snapped at it to test this strange animal's potential. The pup made a slight barking sound, lumbered across the foreshore and slipped quickly over the mud into the water. Once safe in the water, it popped its head up to see what kind of foes we had been.

The owner of *Bawdsey Belle,* a keen seal watcher, thought the seal pup had been born behind Hemley Point and he had spent some time swimming with it in the river. Unfortunately young men on jet skis decided to roar around in circles in the very shallow water behind Hemley Point. One seal was later found dead, covered in bad scars.

When a new pub was built on the edge of Woodbridge, of timber from French farmhouses, they wanted to call it the 'Deben Seal'. However there was a great outcry because residents in the area said there were no seals in the Deben. In fact there is usually at least one seal in the river every winter, although you only see them occasionally.

I was taken aback one day in November in 2001 when I suddenly saw two miniature seals in the creek. Their heads kept bobbing up as they searched for food. Hold on, there is no such thing as a miniature seal. I don't know who was more surprised, the otters, or myself. Even Belle stood totally still and then looked at me as much as to say, 'What on earth are these?'

When Miss Butler visited us in 1975 she stood at the bedroom window and asked, 'And do the otters still play in the creek?'

Apparently back around 1900 the Butler children used to look out of the windows to watch the otters playing in The Creek in the summer evenings.

Shelduck and an oystercatcher seen on Hemley Point at high tide. The blacker the ooze mud the more food there is for birds. Where the ooze has washed away there is less food in the London clay

Before I spotted the two in the creek the only one I had seen here had been lying dead on the marshes. This was shortly after we had come to live at The Cottage and it had been shot in the head, no doubt by one of the keepers of the Old Estate. In the mid-sixties otters were still being seen around Kirton Creek, on the opposite shore of the river. Then the trail went cold for nearly forty years, until 2000 when there were reports that an otter had been seen swimming off Kyson Point, about three miles up river from us.

I tried to find out whether otters had been introduced back to the River Deben or had returned naturally. I contacted Richard Shooter, who had been Conservation Officer of the Otter Trust for seven years, and he told me that he had never seen one of these shy animals in the wild. The Otter Trust had released a pair of otters at Minsmere, some thirty miles away, sixteen years before. They may have bred and moved down the coast. However a more likely source of these otters had been a pair released in the freshwater Deben about seven years before. A male otter needs many miles of territory, and could have moved down into the tidal Deben.

Richard Shooter told me, 'It is difficult to find otters, you very rarely see one and they are only in pairs to mate so you rarely see two together.' I mentioned that I had seen two recently. Obviously this was as rare as a White Christmas.

Since then I have seen otter tracks around the creek during the winter. In the summer there is so much human activity, including speedboats and jet skis roaring about that the wildlife goes into hiding. In the winter the herons feed along the tide line, lone grey sticks that move around silently. In the summer they mostly find some quiet freshwater ditch free of human activity. There is nothing that disturbs wildlife as much as people on foot and one has to wonder, as the population of this corner of East Suffolk grows, how the wildlife will survive this continual human interference.

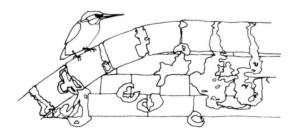

It is amazing how quite large animals can live undetected in the countryside. During the hours of darkness small herds of deer feed freely on the arable crops in the area, but when daylight comes they just vanish from view. Twice, by accident in daylight, I have walked into groups of deer standing silently in woodland. The result was a sudden burst of wild energy as they leaped in the air and galloped off into the distance. Their speed of retreat is their natural way of survival.

There does not appear to have been wild deer in our area since the medieval period, apart from in parkland. It appears that deer escaped from the park at Campsea Ash High House in World War II when the fences were in a poor state. They lived in Tangham Forest and it took about twenty years before they spread out into our parish. A decade later marsh harriers came and nested in the reed beds, perhaps after a gap of forty years. Then badgers, originally from near London, were dumped in the forestry to make way for a housing project. They took about ten years to spread to our parish in the 1990s.

Urban foxes were also dumped in the countryside, and gamekeepers claim that they are tame and easier to shoot! Other birds that have returned are the egrets. During Victorian times they had been shot for their feathers to adorn hats. Spoonbills have also reappeared but it appears that some types of gull have dropped in number. Species keep changing numbers, although often no one really knows the reason.

Some of our new arrivals must have appeared simply because no one wanted them. Our Parish church is in a lonely spot at the end of a public road, a good place to turn out unwanted pets. Over the years we have seen cats, tortoises, guinea fowl and other former pets appear in this area. Perhaps pushed out of a car door just before it departed.

During the harvest in 1999, our combine driver John Leek was surprised to see a 'black cat' about the size of Labrador in the barley at Badley. The big cat, probably a lynx, stayed in the area for several days and appeared to be living quite well on rabbits. Since it did not appear to be frightened by humans we thought it must have either escaped or been released from captivity.

With wildlife one only gets a glimpse of their story, the further chapters remain a mystery. The Badley big cat was part of our lives for several days and then it vanished. About a week later the *East Anglian Daily Times* started to run stories about a big cat being seen about twenty miles away on the Suffolk coastal heaths. Was it the same big cat? We will never know. The only time one of these wildlife mysteries has had a known explanation was when I saw some strange bird by the reeds and reported it to a bird-watching friend.

He rang back, puzzled and said, 'The only bird to fit your description is a flamingo!' Again about two weeks later the local paper had a tiny report about some flamingo, which had escaped from a Dutch zoo, being seen briefly near Clacton. My observations would have sounded ridiculous without these reports.

After one wild winter's gale a buzzard, which should have been a resident of the marshes of Eastern Europe, appeared on the marshes at the far end of our parish. This was closely followed by another species, the all-British bird twitcher, determined to give the unfortunate bird and the residents of the area no peace in their relentless desire for a sighting. When a black-headed warbler, normally found in Greece, appeared in a local garden, a code of local silence fell into place and the twitchers didn't see the bird.

There must always have been birds that have strayed into the wrong territory, but in the past they would have been hunted for the pot or shot for sport. Their survival is probably due to a attitude for conservation in the countryside. The old school of gamekeeper shot everything that was not classified as game.

There must have been a time, in the age of horses and carts, when our parish was as totally silent as the desert. By the standards of southeastern England it is still a quiet place, but once the age of mechanization appeared the sound of tractors became commonplace. As a boy I heard and saw great armadas of American 'silver fortresses' going overhead on missions to bomb Germany. When we first went to live in The Cottage the ear-splitting roar of USAF warplanes was frequent as there were two air bases within a few miles. After the

Cold War ended there was a brief period when the area became quite silent. Then one still summer's evening in 1995 I stood on the hill top (in Suffolk a hill is anything over 50ft high) watching a yacht silently tacking through the Ramsholt moorings and wondered why I could hear a loud thundering noise, like surf breaking on a beach. Another evening I listened again, this time I realised I was hearing traffic noise, but where? I was standing on the edge of a potato field, not a house or road in sight. Suddenly with horror it dawned on me that I was hearing the heavy traffic going to the Port of Felixstowe on the A14 some five miles away on the other side of the river. Since then the roar has grown louder.

Other times, usually in the early hours of the morning or in the dead of night, when the traffic noise dies, we can hear the aeroplanes from London far above us. Once I flew to Oslo, to cover the wonderful wooden boat show at Risor, and the flight went over the East Coast in clear, bright weather. I saw boats on the River Blackwater and yachts on their mooring at West Mersea and then shipping in Harwich Harbour. I was really looking forward to seeing the Deben when we ran into a cloud. I can't complain about the increasing noise as I love travel and must be contributing to it.

It was the same with light pollution. To the east it is still dark, although on clear nights Orfordness lighthouse flashes out a warning beam over the treetops. It was once dark to the west, but now three yellow glows have appeared on the horizon marking Felixstowe, Ipswich and Woodbridge. Woodbridge is the worst of this trinity of light pollution because both the lights from the tennis courts and the football club are clearly visible making an unnatural glow in the night sky. The bright lights of civilisation grow ever closer, but don't bring comfort.

The wildlife does seem to adjust to distant noise and light, but they cannot handle human activity. The whole countryside changes briefly when shooting parties arrive in the district. In the weeks before Christmas, and again at the end of the shooting season we could be living in a war zone. All around our land is gunfire as the great shoots reap the reward of their pheasant and partridge rearing programmes.

Having grown up in the countryside handling a gun was a natural part of life. I started with rabbits and moved on to pheasants. I really enjoyed those superb shoot lunches where, while the bottle was passed around, the rough, dry humour of the farming community told interesting versions of events in the locality. I was not so keen when some of my fellow 'guns' almost shot me. This happened three times.

Once at Alderton Grange the young son of a seed merchant 'followed a low bird through' and fired when it was level with me. I dropped to the ground, and the fence took most of the shot, but I felt a little of it. Another time when cock shooting at the end of season, on a day when the ground was frozen hard, our farm foreman followed a hare through and fired when it was in line with me. This was on an open marsh and there seemed to be a long delay between hearing the report of the gunshot before the pellets hit the ground and ricochet up. Fortunately the shot had travelled a long way before it reached me, but there was a pinging sensation as the pellets hit my body.

An almost fatal time was when walking down a narrow lane in Kettleburgh to the next drive. A gun went off just behind my head and there was the rush of shot over my cap.

I turned in horror to find farmer Moore behind me, who had been used to poaching up the hedges. He had broken the golden rule and was walking between drives with a loaded gun. When a pheasant got up in the lane in front of him he had lifted his gun to fire over my head, a stupid action, but the trigger had caught on a button on his mack and the gun had gone off too soon.

'Blast this old mack,' said the careless old farmer, having nearly killed me, 'they aren't half dangerous'.

I was too shaken to say anything, but from that moment on I wondered about field sports. It didn't seem an attractive proposition to become part of the 'bag' counted at the end of the day. Using a gun to protect crops seemed normal to me, but as I have got older, killing purely for pleasure, has became something I do not wish to be part of.

The Low Light at Harwich. When the Low and High Lighthouses were built in 1814 they lined up to mark the entrance to Harwich Harbour, but shingle coming down the coast has moved Landguard Point south.

Chapter Five

The Unforgiving Waters

When your children start going out into the big wide world it is a very sharp learning experience for any parent. Take the first time our eldest, Caroline, decided to ask two boys home for lunch. This was new territory for me and I was not sure what to talk to seventeen-year-old boys about. I need not have bothered; they did all the talking and quickly pointed out that I had got everything wrong. The meal was nearly over when we looked out of the window and saw a large 68ft motor craft coming straight for The Creek at speed. Close behind it was the police launch *Sir Ian Jacob* trying, it appeared, to offer guidance. The impact of hitting the saltings threw the motor cruiser's bows up into the air.

The two seventeen-year-olds were clearly puzzled by this strange sight and asked, 'Does this happen often?'

'Oh yes,' I replied casually, feeling that I had temporarily regained the high ground. When the tide went down a bit I went out to talk to our unexpected visitor. Climbing on to the unpainted decks I joined the lone occupant in the bare wheelhouse. He explained that he lived in Halifax and his wife had kicked him out, but he felt that if he could get a boat to Hull then his son would want to see him there. The plan was OK so far, but after he bought the boat at Woodbridge and set out for Hull things started to go sadly wrong.

In the four miles since he had left Woodbridge he had been aground on the mud several times. He only had a road map for a navigational aid, and the river police had tried to persuade him not to make the voyage. I suggested that the police had been offering good advice.

Our newly arrived neighbour was not put off so easily. I tried another tack and talked about the difficulties of crossing the Deben bar and the tide races off Orfordness. The motor craft owner looked at his road map and since none of these things were marked did not appear to think they would be a problem. He intended to call at Lowestoft and was very keen to know whether you turned left or right once you got in the harbour. His map was not a large scale one and didn't mark such details.

For a month, until the next high spring tide, he was our neighbour, but we saw little of him. Occasionally we saw a lone figure wandering off up the river wall to get stores. Then once again, the police launch turned up to offer more advice, and this time he got further down river before ploughing up on the mud in front of the 'Ramsholt Arms' for another month's stay. I wonder if he ever reached Hull. We all have a promised land to seek in life, and I have noticed that people with absolutely no knowledge of the sea sometimes achieve the most incredible voyages because it does not occur to them how difficult it can be.

Jonathan's first solo trip fell into that category. When Caroline wanted to learn to sail we bought her *Cockle,* a rather elderly Mirror dinghy. Jonathan, at thirteen, was already

Home from sailing.

totally committed to wooden traditional boats and never displayed any interest in the Mirror. I set out to find him the oldest possible wooden boat. The hunt led to a garden near the Ipswich by-pass, I think the boat owner was delighted to think someone was foolish enough to purchase his ancient 12ft clinker, lugsail dinghy.

We named her *Little Wonder* because, although she leaked in numerous places, she sailed very well. We had a few trial sails and then Jonathan asked if he could go out with his school friend Martin Yardley. I said, 'Just stay in sight' and then, after these famous last words, I was very surprised when they just sailed off into the distance.

This was at 10am and by lunchtime there was still no sign of them. Pearl and Caroline walked along the river wall to the Tips to try and find them, but I kept saying I felt they would be all right.

In the back of my mind was the memory of a few years earlier when on a similar cold spring day I found a new red Mirror dinghy, with its sails still set, sitting at the mouth of the creek. That empty Mirror is one of the saddest sights I have ever seen. The young woman had been out on her first sail in her new Mirror, recently bought at the Boat Show. Her father had been waiting down river at The Dock for her to return. The other boating men said she had been gone a long time and he should call out the lifeboat. The father seemed sure 'she can handle it', but she never came back and they planted a wood in her memory in Hollesley.

Back at The Creek the whole day was spent in a mixture of despair and anxiety. Where were the boys? I was working on *L'Atalanta* and managed to kick over a tin of paint, this is a tradition I have managed to keep up most seasons, but it does not improve my temper.

Shooting the herring drifting nets on the *Three Sisters*. 2003.

Hauling the herring nets on the *Three Sisters*. 2003.

When the tide went down I worked on the side of *L'Atalanta,* but the ladder slowly capsized sideways and dropped me into the cold wet mud.

At 4pm I spotted the tiny sail of *Little Wonder* fighting her way back down river. It turned out that the boys had really not heard my 'stay in sight' advice, which had sounded a bit dull to them, and they had run at speed all the way up river to Woodbridge. Here they had a long chat with Frank Knights, bought an ice cream and it came as a complete surprise to find how difficult it was to beat back against the wind.

Jonathan and Martin's sailing partnership lasted over ten years and ended when they got in real trouble. The first we knew was when Clare, Jonathan's wife, called on the mobile to say, 'They are both all right and the helicopter has landed Martin on Waldringfield beach'. What was going on!

We had bought the 15ft open gaff rigged winkle brig *Mary Agnes*. A good sailer, but we did not know about her strange habit of burying her bows in strong winds. Anyway Jonathan and Martin went for a sail on a cold spring evening. There was plenty of wind and when hit by a squall the *Mary Agnes* simply sailed under. She had buoyancy tanks, but there had been an oyster dredge in the boat (we had tried to find oysters in the Deben) and this had fallen out and anchored the boat to the bottom. Clinging on to the side, Martin chose this moment to remark that he did not swim.

They both had lifejackets, but the heavy boat was anchored in deep water on the sort of evening no other boats were in sight or likely to be. Many people would have panicked and drowned at this point, but Jonathan was in his home waters. He could see the lights of his own house. He knew where the tide would take him; it took an hour to reach the mud then to scramble up and run home to summons help.

A summer's Sunset over The Creek.

Jonathan and Harry hauling the shrimp trawl on the *Mary Amelia* before the cabin was removed. 2003.

The Deben is such a beautiful river it is difficult to realise that it can, particularly when the water is cold, be a death trap. I know a whole list of people who have ended their days in the waters of this most wonderful river. Best known was the artist John Western, whose untimely end one foggy day at Kyson Point is still deeply mourned by many people. The last tragedy in the spring of 2003 was when we were bringing 34ft *Mary Amelia* back from a visit to the boatyard. Off Methersgate Quay we saw an elderly man going up river in a dinghy powered by an outboard. We waved and he gave us a casual wave back. He must have gone by the time we picked up our mooring. Later that afternoon his body had been taken ashore at Kyson Point.

I have fallen in the Deben twice. The first time was in 1959, in the Ramsholt Reach. In those days it was still open water, before all the moorings choked up the channel, but in spite of having the whole river we managed, on a hot summer afternoon in *Sea Fever,* to drift down alongside a boat that was anchored for angling. No damage, no problem, I just pushed the two boats apart and then fell straight down between them. I went under *Sea Fever,* the only time I ever saw her bottom while she was in the water, and came up behind the dinghy and hauled myself in.

For some strange reason, young men don't do sensible things; I was wearing thigh boots, not a wise move. I decided to learn from this experience, as I hate being in the water, and haven't worn thigh boots afloat again. I went a step further and always wore boots a size too large so that if I ever fell in again I could kick them off.

I had worn several pairs of boots out before, over forty years later, I put this theory to the test, and it worked. We had been out to try and photograph the barque *Endeavour* coming into Harwich Harbour. This had proved a waste of time, it was raining and blowing hard and we hadn't left the Deben. Back on the mooring we were keen to get ashore as it was still raining hard. Jonathan said he would row so I got into the dinghy, and as I sat in the stern all the water in the dinghy ran towards me and I just rolled gently backwards into the river with surprising ease, holding my expensive camera equipment in a bag.

My first thoughts were to try and save my camera bag but the salt water must have ruined everything before I got it back in the dinghy. Later I spent months arguing with my insurance company over how I fell in, but actually it was very easy. At twenty-two I had hauled myself out of the water, but at sixty-five, even with a special waterproof jacket that kept me afloat, I could not haul myself out of the water. Something in me said, 'Stay calm and think absolutely logically'.

I swam to the side of *Mary Amelia,* which from water level looked like the *QEII.* I asked Jonathan to put a rope under my shoulders and he hauled me back aboard on the backstay block and tackle.

I have found it difficult to admit that I had ever been foolish enough to have fallen in, but have since discovered that many of my boating friends 'of a certain age' had fallen in under similar circumstances, but did not want it to become public knowledge. It is very hard to admit you have been in difficulties.

In 1994 we took the *Three Sisters,* then freshly rebuilt, to her first East Coast Old Gaffers Race. It was a day of calm peaceful winds but in the early evening the wind picked up making the boats anchored off Stone Point bob about in the River Blackwater. The smack *Mermaid's* boat put out from shore with six people aboard. Once out in the river the overloaded smack's boat hit the popple, filled and rolled over putting everyone in the water.

The little group clinging to the up turned boat drifted off down the Blackwater. We dashed out to their assistance, hauled some of them out, one by one, up over the bows and returned them, wet and shaken, to safety. On shore we saw them all again, no one spoke to us or even seemed to notice we were there. It is embarrassing to be rescued and people just want to forget the whole incident.

Chapter Six

Legends of the East

On the lower part of the River Blackwater there is a post marking the end of a muddy spit known as The Nass. When coming in from the sea this post is often difficult to pick out against the high ground, but when leaving West Mersea it stands proud and is easy to spot.

The Nass, one of the corruptions of the Norse word, ness, for a headland, also marks the entrance to a series of creeks that splinter off through the marshes. If you like muddy creeks this part of the world is heaven, if you don't like them, you are missing half the appeal of the East Coast.

One of the places reached by passing the Nass post is Tollesbury. It is a large village overlooking a vast flat stretch of marsh with Mersea Island visible in the distance. Once half the men in Tollesbury made a living from fishing with smacks, but those days are long gone. There was still plenty of yachting activity in 2004, but Ben Rigby was the only fisherman working commercially, when there were fish about.

The golden age of working sailing craft of the Victorian and Edwardian era still casts its shadow over the creeks of Essex. Most villages still have a few restored sailing smacks. The fishermen from the Rivers Blackwater and Colne, because they went yachting in the summer, loved a fast smack. These smacks were built in the same yards as the Victorian yachts and took on many of their qualities. To understand the smacks, and how they should be kept, it helps to know about the working life of the men who sailed them.

When we bought an old 12ft smack's boat from Steve Hall he told us it had been built by Frost and Drake at Tollesbury. It was not difficult to work out who had been the original owners because, 'K & W Musset' was carved in the stern. People at Tollesbury said 'that's 'Navvy's' old boat!' and the owner of *Lamplighter* said 'when ever I went past 'Navvy's' place you could always smell smoked fish, I liked that.'

We named our boat *Musset,* which seemed an obvious choice, and I got in contact with Keith Mussett. He and his father Walter, who had always been known as 'Walt' by his family and 'Navvy' by the fishermen, had had the boat built in 1952 by 'Curly' Drake. The smacks had always towed a 13ft boat, which worked well for sprat fishing in the winter, but they had been a 'damn nuisance shrimp trawling in the summer because they were always banging about alongside'. Keith also told me that they had ordered a slightly smaller boat than normal because the older boats were so heavy to drag down the beach.

No one was quite sure whether our boat was one used by 'Navvy' in the 1953 Floods. Certainly when this huge tide came surging up the Tollesbury Fleets 'Navvy' Mussett and three other fishermen decided to row from Woodrolfe Creek and make sure that their smacks were safe at The Leavings. This mission didn't go as planned. The tide proved far stronger than they realised and the boat, loaded with fishermen, was swept right over the top of the river wall and down on to the flooded marshes.

Keith Mussett was fourteen when he started shrimp fishing with Uriah Lewis on the smack *Lucy*. There were then about sixteen boats working from Tollesbury, but he produced a list of 108 smacks that had been owned there in about 1919. By 1940 the remaining smacks had all been fitted with engines and worked from The Fleets, the creek above Mersea Quarters, but they landed their catch at Woodrolfe Creek.

Harry pumping out on *Mary Amelia* with the *Musset* astern. The deck pump was originally out of a Lowestoft smack.

Originally coal being brought to Tollesbury was landed at the head of the Fleets, at Old Hall, but in about 1850 the granary was built on stilts on Woodrolfe Creek, a smaller side creek. Although over shadowed by modern sheds the granary on stilts still sits by Woodrolfe Creek, while similar sheds at Landermere, Woodbridge, Melton and Iken have long since gone. The old style East Coast, of sail and sweat, has been replaced by international container ships and an increasing tide of mass-produced yachts. Some places have changed completely but others, like Woodrolfe Creek, have just changed a little.

Keith Mussett at Woodrolfe Creek, Tollesbury.

The name Woodrolfe is a corruption of the place where 'wood came up'. This was timber, on brigs, from the Baltic. The first name was Woodrow but this was corrupted into Woodrolfe Creek, but the smackmen always called it the original 'Wood Up Creek'.

After he had been shrimping Keith Mussett joined Uriah Lewis' 21ton 47ft smack *My Alice* for the winter 'stowboating' for sprat. The 'stow' or stall net was a medieval invention evolved because there was not enough room to use a drift net in the narrow Thames Estuary channels. The fishermen used to watch out for the seagulls diving on the sprat shoals and anchored their smacks just down tide of them before lowering their huge triangular nets down into the water. They didn't just get sprat, many other kinds of fish went into the nets, but these were sold separately.

The stowboaters followed the shoals of sprat, off Sheerness, in the Swin or the 'Wellit' (Wallet) channels. In 1941 Navvy Mussett was on wartime Yacht Patrol and he spotted that the Thames was full of sprat. He rigged up a smoke house in the fort at Cliff Foot in the Lower Hope, and reported back to Tollesbury that the shoals were in the mouth of the Thames. The Lower Hope was not really a very healthy place to fish because 'Bovril Boats' were discharging there. These were the ships which normally pumped raw London sewage out in the Thames Estuary, but one had been sunk by a mine.

That winter the *My Alice* and other Tollesbury boats were stowboating in the Lower Hope and landed their sprat at Tilbury or Gravesend. When the smacks landed at Gravesend, food shortages had already started and the queues outside the fishmongers used to be all the way down the street and round the corner. Clearly no one mentioned the 'Bovril Boats'.

Five men on the *My Alice* were all paid on a share of the catch, but she was still a popular smack because she was larger than most and could land 12-14 tons, making her a good earner. The next winter he joined Joe Heard's 44ft *Iris Mary* for stowboating off the Essex coast.

John Brett's rebuilt smack *Iris Mary* at the Aldous Heritage Smack Dock, Brightlingsea, 2004.

As World War II was in full cry the Essex boats with their trawls and stow nets were effectively 'minesweeping' with predictable results. Herbert Stoker and his wife were blown up in their West Mersea smack, and a Harwich boat was also blown up. The Tollesbury *Rosena* 'caught' a mine trawling, but was lucky. While the crew pumped the *Sunbeam* towed them into Brightlingsea. The *Thistle* also got a mine in the trawl but the explosion sank her.

In 1941 the Tollesbury smack *Alpha* hit a mine, but although damaged she managed to get back home. Later that year the smack *Express* was sunk by a mine and her crew rowed ashore in a duck punt they had on the foredeck. The owner bought the Leigh bawley *Grace* and renamed her *Little Express,* only to be hit by another mine when all three men aboard were killed. Keith's brother Bernard was one of the men lost and after this his mother persuaded him to come ashore and work in a rigger's loft, but he hated it and wanted to 'get back in the boats.'

The fo'c'sle of the bawley *Saxonia,* an original cabin layout from the working era. The skippers loved a fast boat, but the crews looked for a comfortable fo'c'sle.

Keith regarded the tea Tollesbury smackmen drank almost as dangerous as the German war effort! The smackmen put their tea, condensed milk and sugar into the kettle and boiled it up, they then poured the strong brew straight into old cups. Keith and the aged skipper Lewis had preferred a weaker brew.

In 1948 two Leigh brothers started trawling for sprat with the Danish Larsen pair trawls and after this only a few smacks with low powered engines continued stowboating for a few more years. The summer shrimping was also declining and many Essex boats switched to white weeding. There had long been a little trade in dredging up weed from the seabed and it was sold, dyed, for household decorations. In the early 1950s this became a sudden boom, and there were men at Leigh who sold their houses to buy boats for white weeding.

Keith Mussett went white weeding in the *William & Emily* from Tollesbury and several of the West Mersea boats were also fitted out with huge dredges. It was a real 'gold rush', once the Mussetts got so much valuable white weed that, rather than throw it away, they paid the crew of the Barrow lightship to store it until they came back. In her best week the *William & Emily* earned her crew £160 each. This was at a time when most men would have been pleased with £7 at the end of the week. Keith went to Scotland and bought a new boat.

Keith Mussett, like many longshore fishermen, also went into the merchant navy 'to see the world.' He also took part in the Essex practice of being a yacht skipper during the summer. In 1958 he was part of the crew on the 12-metre *Sceptre* in the America Cup

Jim Lawrence hauling the first of the season's oysters with the Mayor of Colchester, Chris Hall on the bawley *Saxonia,* 2003. This traditional opening 'gin and gingerbread' ceremony of Colchester oyster fishery dates back to 1540.

challenge, 'We knew she was no good' he summed up that challenge. Ten years later he gave up fishing, 'It was a good life, but no money in it.' He sold his boat and started a successful engineering business.

It took quite a lot of diplomacy, and most of one winter to buy, the boat *Musset.* She was one of only about four genuine Essex smack's boats left. We lived in Suffolk and there was some discussion about whether this prime piece of Essex maritime heritage should go over the border into a Suffolk river. However we were considered trustworthy enough to take on this leaky piece of the East Coast maritime past. On the East Coast these things are very important. However when the great revival of interested in traditional sailing craft started on this coast none were more surprised than the men who had once sailed these craft for a living.

When Headley Farrington had been the manager of the Francis and Gilders barge fleet at Colchester, he had been responsible for taking the sailing gear out of their last sailing barges. In about 1955 the barges, *Mirosa, Dawn* and many more, were taken up to the yard, one by one, and all the sailing gear was taken out of them. As Headley could not think what to do with a great pile of old sails, rigging and spars, he had them burnt. A decade later Headley was constantly being asked if he had any old sailing gear. By this time he could have sold the lot to the enthusiasts who were rigging out sailing barges.

The barge *Mirosa* passing the Container ship *Cosco Singapore* of Hong Kong, 2004. Water transport, a century apart, at the Port of Felixstowe.

The generations of men who worked the traditional craft of the coast may have almost gone, but they have not been forgotten. One Saturday in January 1967 I met Harold Smy in the 'Lord Nelson', a pub just back from the waterfront at Ipswich Dock. Harold was the skipper of Raymond Sully's barge *Beatrice Maud* and had returned home for the weekend while his barge was being discharged at Great Yarmouth. Harold was one of the older and more respected skippers, a position he greatly enjoyed, and was in good form telling up tales of his long life working in barges on the coast.

One of his first freights had been back in the 1920s in a little barge called *Cryalls*. He had gone around to load wheat at Landermere Quay in Walton Backwater. When he arrived he walked up to the farmhouse and was told that the wheat was still growing in the field. In interwar years freights were often difficult to get so Harold waited. The farmer lent him a gun and he went around the farm shooting rabbits. After the wheat was cut, threshed and the barge finally loaded, he sailed the few miles to the mills at Ipswich.

Another difficult freight to a creek wharf was in the Butley River when he was asked to take shingle from the river mouth at Shingle Street up to Chillesford Lodge where new stables were being built for polo ponies. The Shingle Street men helped them to load the shingle with the special wheelbarrows that they pushed up planks. There was an art in doing this because if you got out of step the wheelbarrow was thrown over the side. Once loaded Harold took his barge up the River, which is very shallow above Gedgrave Cliff, and they were only able to move forward a short distance on the top of each tide. It took a week to cover the last few reaches and Harold and his mate were very fed up by the time they arrived.

The owner of the stables was also unhappy at the time it had taken for the first freight to be delivered. He had come down to the barge and said, 'Well skipper, I hope you are not going to take so long next time!'

'There is not going to be a next time,' said young Harold, 'the rest of your shingle is going up to Rope's Quay at Orford!'

In the village that one freight was soon forgotten, only Harold remembered it because it had been so difficult. It was the tail end of an era when there had been considerable trade to small wharves and hards in the most unlikely places. On the Deben, which is only about seven miles long, there were at least nineteen places where barges had handled cargoes in the nineteenth century.

Thames barges and smacks could have faded out in the early 1960s, when their original use finished, and their hulls left to rot away in lonely creeks. Before this people had been buying up old workboats, to get cheap yachts, and when they wore out they had been abandoned. It was the younger men, fired by the nostalgia for the golden age of sail, who put tremendous energy into keeping the old vessels going. A new era began when John Fairbrother said he was rebuilding his barge *Kitty* so that she would 'last into the next century' and Mike Frost totally rebuilt his beloved 1808 smack *Boadicea* at Tollesbury.

Faversham smack *Emeline* at dawn off Brightlingsea.

In the spring of 2003 we attended a tense meeting of the Sailing Smack Association aboard the sailing barge *Glenway* at the Hythe Quay, Maldon, the very heart of the East Coast traditional boat movement. There was a kind of agreement that if an old workboat is taken to pieces and an exact copy is built in the same 'air space' then it is in the same boat. The point at issue was, that as we grew further away from the age of working sail, some smacks were beginning to look like modern racing yachts. It was suggested at this meeting that smacks with hollow spars should carry a heavier handicap when racing. Since most of the keen racers had hollow spars there were some sharp comments from the back.

The following summer saw the East Coast smack world in turmoil as the racing men battled it out with those who wished to keep their boats in an absolutely traditional form. The traditionalists said that smacks and bawleys should stay as near as possible to their original state.

Totally restoring a workboat is an extremely expensive project to undertake. Over the years I have met and reported the activities of hundreds of these determined people, and have great admiration for them. Behind many rebuilds are stories of broken marriages and relationships, promising careers abandoned and heavy debts incurred. I vowed to learn from other people's mistakes and never become involved with the restoration of a large traditional craft. If only I had stuck to this wise advice I would have saved a lot of time and money!

The first boat we restored was the 15ft *Pet,* which we found rotting away on Thorpeness beach. A decade later we had another sailing Suffolk beach boat, the 18ft *Three Sisters,* rebuilt in the shape of the original 1896 clinker hull. In spite of much advice from the many experts, who came in the builder's shed, we kept to the original layout and dipping lug rig. I felt I had done my bit towards the traditional boat restoration, saved an endangered boat type, but then I drifted into the Dawn Sailing Barge Trust.

The 82ft *Dawn* was built by Walter Cook at Maldon in 1897 for the 'stackie trade', taking hay and straw to London to feed the street horses and cows kept in city barns. In the second half of the nineteenth century this was a booming trade around the Thames Estuary. Just about every creek had a farm wharf, in Suffolk they were called 'docks', where barges came in to load mangolds in the hold and straw and hay. They built stacks on their decks that went half way up the mainmast.

The *Dawn* has a beamy hull and low sides because the stack freight was bulky but light. She was a successful stackie barge and is reputed to have been the only Maldon barge to have never lost a stack on the way to the Thames. It must have been a special kind of seamanship to be able to sail a barge with a stack halfway up the mast. The mate had to stand on top of the stack and shout directions to the skipper.

Once, at night, in about 1900 one of Wrinch's stackie barges ran into a small yacht that had been anchored at the Stone Heaps, at the entrance to the river Orwell. The yacht got jammed across the barge's bow and was taken down Harwich Harbour with the skipper, aft, totally unaware that it was there. The youngest member of the yacht crew was told to hurry up and climb over the barge's bow and stack to warn the skipper. When he appeared out of the darkness beside him the poor man was so surprised he nearly had a heart attack.

The barges returned from London to the farms and villages with freights of muck. These muck freights must have almost been the undoing of the *Dawn* as the hull was so rotten that she was taken back to Cook's yard, Maldon in 1927 and rebuilt. When they put

Cooks yard, on the left, with sailing barges lying at the Hythe Quay, Maldon, 2004

Sara and the swans at Maldon with Cook's yard in the middle.

in a new keelson they sank the barge and floated the new one in through the barge's bow. She was rebuilt again just after World War II, so that she could be loaded with timber, another freight that was also stacked on deck.

The *Dawn's* skipper for many years was 'Hobby' Keeble and he was extremely uncertain how to manoeuvre under power when the first engine was fitted in the barge. They kept the engine running the whole way to London, but as they approached the docks 'Hobby' began to lose his nerve so he stopped the engine and went in under sail.

After many adventures the *Dawn* ended up in a dilapidated state in a boat yard at Hoo on the River Medway. All around the *Dawn* were the hulls of other barges which had gone there to be rebuilt and never left. So why save the *Dawn?* Just about all the surviving barges are the big coasting types, fine barges, but the low-sided *Dawn* was one of the last real stackie barges, a true East Coast craft.

When I became the Trust's chairman neither the barge nor the Trust had a very bright future. We spent the first years fighting off a series of legal claims, and there was no money to do anything about the barge. Things got going when Neil and Stuart Holdsworth were given the 240 gross ton coaster *Johno*. She was a much newer ship than *Dawn,* having been built for the Rhine grain trade in 1961 and had later worked between Galway and the Aran Islands, but her career as a ballast barge on the East Coast had been a chequered one. After she sank in the River Colne the harbour master said that The Trust could have the *Johno* so long as she never returned to 'his' river.

The *Johno* was towed over to the River Medway to be turned into a dry dock. Blocks were placed in the hold and then holes cut in the side so that she would sink into Hoo Creek. In fact the *Johno* refused to sink and more holes had to be cut until suddenly she sank like a stone. The *Dawn* was towed in and as the tide went down she settled into the *Johno's* hold on the blocks. On the next low tide the holes in *Johno's* sides were welded up and she floated with the barge sitting safely in the hold.

The whole exercise was carried out brilliantly, even if the Medway Conservancy did go bananas when they heard some barge enthusiast had sunk a coaster in one of their creeks. However by that time the *Johno* and *Dawn* were on their way being towed across the Thames Estuary back to the barge's old homeport of Maldon. Here the scruffy pair received a very guarded welcome. The *Dawn* had become a very different barge to the one that had undertaken charter work from the Hythe Quay for many years.

It was the aim of the Trust to rebuild her so that she could go on sailing for a second century. For a long time the Trust did not have enough cash to start the serious rebuild.

Gerrard Swift took members of the Trust for trips on the barge *Cabby* which were great morale boosters and two Maldon councillors, Boyce and Mead, became supporters of our rebuild project. By this time we were battling with filling in the Heritage Lottery forms, an art form in itself, to try and get a grant.

There was a tremendous day when we received a phone call saying, 'Congratulations the Heritage Lottery has decided to back the rebuilding of the *Dawn.*' Berthing the barge cost £750 a month so we were very keen to move on quickly with the rebuild, but the Lottery kept asking for more and more detailed costings and reports.

We battled on, the Trustees putting their own money in to keep the Trust going. As chairman, the more time and effort I put into *Dawn* the harder it was to think of giving up. We had no sooner solved one problem when there were two more threatening to close us down.

The sailing barge *Dawn* arriving at Heybridge Basin after the *Johno* had been partly cut down into a dry dock.

Members of the Dawn Sailing Barge Trust cleaning out the barge *Dawn* at Heybridge. All the junk was passed up the line and over the bow.

All the time the barge was deteriorating and the costs rising. Time went by and many supporters, because nothing was happening, became disenchanted. The seven on the committee battled on, and eventually it was the Maldon MP John Whittingdale who saved the day. He went to see the head of the Lottery and enquired why it was all taking so long. The Lottery suddenly reacted, and almost at once things started to happen. Three years after the initial phone call Tim Goldsack was allowed to start the rebuild at Heybridge Basin. The lengthy delays had about doubled the cost of the rebuild, but without the Heritage Lottery Grant we could never have started.

Some people find degenerating barge hulks very romantic. My grandson Harry, for one, is greatly attracted to old rotting barges. It was in search of a barge wreck that we set off for Kirton Creek in my lugger *Three Sisters*. We had to wait for high tide to get up the creek and then we passed right over the top of the wreck. It was a case of *Three Sisters* going over the barge *Three Sisters*. Looking down into the water we could just see the outline of the hull and windlass of the Maldon barge *Three Sisters*. She had been built in 1865 and had been worn out when she had come into Kirton Creek with a freight of muck for the farms. She was in such bad order that the crew left and walked home to Ipswich. The barge eventually sank out in the creek and the local watermen came in and robbed her of all useful gear.

Later I suggested we should look at another barge hulk, the 83ft *Westall* that was up at Melton. Again we had to wait for near high water to get to the wreck. I remembered seeing the *Westall* come into the river from Southwold, on her last sea going trip, in 1985. It had been a still winter's Sunday and even then her end was predictable. She had already been converted to a houseboat and had a large tent on the foredeck.

Tim Goldsack with the first planks in the rebuild of the barge *Dawn,* He started at the bottom and worked up, 2004.

Melton's houseboat colony was a very emotive subject, many local people fought to have them removed while the houseboat owners stayed firmly in their berths. The problem was that when the boats sank they were abandoned, this happened to the *Westall* and there was a tremendous row when she was deliberately set on fire to get rid of her.

The fire brigade was called and insisted on putting out the fire, while many wanted her burnt. We visited the charred remains of the *Westall* out on the ooze near Flea Island, a patch of saltings below Melton Station. During the previous winter I had been involved with overwhelming problems to keep the *Dawn* Project going, but at least by fighting on perhaps the *Dawn* will have a new life and not end up like the barges *Three Sisters* or *Westall*.

Back in about 1968 the 48ft barge *Cygnet* was up for sale for £450 and I went to see her on the hard at Pin Mill. She was in a poor state; in one place I did my own survey by pushing my hand right through the rotten timbers. I didn't have the money or skill to rebuild her, but I felt strongly that I should save at least one barge.

Pin Mill after some of the barge wrecks had been cleared away, 2003.

The *Cygnet* had been built in 1881 at the time when the trade to farm wharves was at its height. She carried wheat from the farm wharves on the Rivers Orwell and Stour to the mills at Ipswich and Felixstowe. The *Cygnet* is a half size barge, with the mast stepped well forward, and I never thought that she looked right until I saw her loaded with a stack at Snape Maltings Quay in 2003. This was part of Des Kaliszewski's project to re-enact some of the old barge customs. Loaded with a stack, and bricks in the hold, the *Cygnet* looked just right.

Des has spent a lifetime skippering barges and sailing his own boats. The most notable was in 1987 when he sailed around the British Isles single-handed. This voyage was not made in a light-weight modern yacht, but the heavily rigged Danish fishing ketch *Sylvanna Suzanna*.

One brisk May morning I was walking back down the lane with Belle when I was amazed to see the topmast of a barge, over The Cottage roof. I knew at once this could only be Des sailing the *Cygnet* into The Creek.

Des Kaliszewski hauling the barge *Cygnet* out of The Creek, 2004.

The most vital part of any book is the front cover. All winter I had been trying to take photographs of the otters, but after hours spent watching I hadn't seen them again. When I saw *Cygnet's* topmast I knew this was the answer to my problem. With boats you have to grab the moment quickly or the opportunity has gone. I ran for my camera so that I could record this moment.

Since Des is a single-handed sailor he cruises in the winter because there are no yachts about and he can leave the tiller for a short time while he handles the sails. The previous winter he had revived an old scene by sailing into many East Coast Rivers with a 'stackie' freight. On the River Blackwater he had sailed up a Northey Island creek to the farm in the middle. The National Trust representative was horrified that a barge had suddenly appeared right in amongst what was regarded as being the sole preserve of birds.

The barge *Cygnet* at Snape Maltings, loaded with a stack freight, 2003.

Des also sailed up Ray Creek, off the River Colne, to the old jetty where, between about 1930 and 1957, Samuel West barges used to go and load shingle from Colne Point. The Ray Creek continues to bend around behind Colne Point to St Osyth's beach. Here on the exposed Essex marshland is the ultimate creek village of Lee over Sands. This scattered group of houses, two miles down a farm track, are actually a failed holiday resort, started by a company in about 1932. The airstrip and golf course are long gone and the tennis courts have reverted back to saltings.

Lee over Sands overlooks the top of the Ray Creek with the beach beyond.

Lee over Sands is just behind Colne Point.

Outside the river wall overlooking Ray Creek are thirteen low houses on stilts, which developed from the 1930s beach huts. On one visit Malcolm told us he had lived in one of the flat roofed bungalows beside the creek for four years. In the winter it had been very bleak, a high tide covers the track leaving the bungalows a series of tiny islands in angry tidal water. Malcolm's was one of the older bungalows, built of wood, and in the winter it was very difficult to keep warm. Yet he loved the isolation and at Easter, when the first walkers appeared, he felt the place was being invaded.

The visit by Des to Ray Creek in *Cygnet* was part of his plan to visit, under sail, as many old 'stackie' wharves as possible. On his trip to the River Deben he had already visited Wilford Wharf, Ramsholt and Hemley Docks, none of which had been used by barges since the 1920s, but our creek was too small for a barge berth so this was probably the first time a barge had ever been there. This did not seem to bother the single-handed barge sailor he had just enjoyed visiting The Creek. Occasionally the clock is turned back and images from old black and white photographs come to life.

Harry on the remains at the 1865 Maldon barge *Three Sisters* in Kirton Creek.

Chapter Seven

Black and White Photographs

I had the weird feeling I was stepping back in time, into a wartime photograph. Walking along the quay at Whitstable there was a party of World War II naval ratings who had stopped to chat to some girls in 1940s skirts and their hair done up in buns. When I was a small boy people dressed like this, my mother had a tweed skirt very similar to the one worn by the first girl to reach the Unit Canteen Van. On the quay one of actors was pacing about learning his lines for the next round of filming once the break was over. After the break Jonathan and I returned to his cockler *Mary Amelia* and we steamed out of the harbour behind the other boats to take part in the filming of the BBC2 documentary drama 'Dunkirk'.

I suppose this is the nearest I will ever get to the 1940 Dunkirk Evacuation of British troops from the beaches of northern France, but I can just remember hearing about it at the time. One of my uncles, John Garrard, the owner of the *Lassie,* was in the Royal Marines and his boat was sunk at Dunkirk. There was great relief when he came back. John Garrard learnt to swim in Hollesley Bay and had spent two hours in the water at Dunkirk before being rescued. All around him men were screaming as they fought for their lives. A battle most of them lost. John Garrard's only comment was that if only they had learnt to swim properly, or even just learnt to keep afloat, most of them would have survived. He also took part in the D-Day landings on the beaches of Normandy and summed up the whole thing by saying 'they go on about the War, but I just came home and got on with my life. Nobody talked about therapy in those days'.

The Miracle of Dunkirk was that although this had been a humiliating defeat with the German Nazi army having blitzed its way through France driving all before it. Enough members of the British Army had got home to reform and fight on. This retreat was achieved partly with the help with small boats from the East Coast of England. Naval officers had gone around the waterside areas asking for boats to go on an 'important mission.' At Felixstowe Ferry Charlie Brinkley had just come in from shrimping in the *Silver Cloud* when he was 'asked' to report to Ramsgate. Up at Woodbridge, Frank Knights was working at Robertson's boatyard when he was asked to go and crew on *L'Atalanta* 'on a mission'. The *Silver Cloud* and *L'Atalanta* left the Deben together, their crews having to guess where they were going. They went across to Ramsgate where the ships were being assembled. From here they set out for the French coast, but after about two hours steaming a Royal Navy vessel came up to them and said it was all over and they should go back.

George Osborne, on the other hand, came very close to being a casualty of the Dunkirk Evacuation. He was part of the working crew of his father's Leigh cockler *Renown*, which, with five other cocklers, were ordered straight to Dunkirk. Because George had a bad arm, he was left behind. The cocklers left Old Leigh at 8am and steamed out of the Thames Estuary and across the southern North Sea. On the way over, German aircraft tried to sink them, and when they arrived at Dunkirk they found that all hell had been let loose and the whole town was under bombardment. The six Leigh cocklers ferried around 1,000 soldiers from the harbour out to waiting ships. Some of the Leigh men went ashore on Dunkirk Mole, just to say they had been 'to France'. They had worked in the Thames Estuary all their lives and had never been that far away before.

Dawn at the Red Sands Towers, 2003.

In the evening the six boats set out for home, but Osborne's *Renown* had trouble with her engine and asked Dench's *Lettita* for a tow. They were nearly back when a mine bumped along the bottom of *Lettita* and then blew up the *Renown* with all three Leigh men and one naval rating aboard her. On the *Lettita* they just pulled the towrope in and that was all they ever found.

George and his father were in the barber's shop when someone rushed in with the news that the boats were back, but the *Renown* had gone in one terrible explosion.

When we met George Osborne he was most keen to talk about his days in the *Mary Amelia*. This sailing cockler, named after his grandmother, had been built for his father in 1914. The builder was Heyward, a Deal man who had moved to Southend in the 1880s because there was a demand for shallow draft boats to work off the foreshore. The *Mary Amelia* was launched in an appropriate way for a cockler, built to work on the sands. She was towed down the road by a traction engine and left on the foreshore to float on the tide. After World War I the Heyward Works were building shallow draft motorboats that were towed down to the water by an old wartime tank they had bought.

George said 'I felt sorry for him, Bill Heyward built good boats, but the poor sod went bankrupt'.

The cockle-raking scene during the filming of the BBC2 'Dunkirk' with the Gravelines trawler *Christ Roi*. When the past is recreated it always comes out a little different to the original.

George was born the day the *Mary Amelia* was launched and had a tremendously strong attachment to the boat. We asked him about cockling under sail in the 1920s. They left Old Leigh at high water and sailed out to one of the sandbanks in the Thames Estuary. ' We knew where to go' said George.

John Dench with *Lettita* nearly lost his life looking for the cockle beds. Once, on his own, he ran aground on Foulness and was walking about with a stick, poking for cockles, when he suddenly saw a bank of fog rolling over the flat empty sands. He ran as hard as he could for the *Lettita,* if he had lost sight of her it could have been fatal. Fortunately he reached his boat before the fog totally engulfed him.

The boats were run ashore where the cockle beds appeared, on the Main, Maplin, Pollock or wherever, then they waited for low water so that the men could hand rake the cockles out of the sands. If they couldn't find enough cockles they worked a 'double tide', and stayed out there for another twelve hours. When George spoke of the banks in the Thames Estuary he used the old names. Marsh End off Canvey was 'Mush End' the Red Sands was 'Reds'n' and so on.

Because of the handwork there were normally large crews on the cocklers, usually four men were carried on sailing cocklers while the later motor cocklers had up to eight. After filling the hold the men slept down in the forepeak. On the 34ft *Mary Amelia,* the forepeak was very small, but two men slept on the lockers on either side while the rest lay on the floor between them. George, a small man and then just a teenager, slept forward of the bitts' right up in the bow. There were no unnecessary luxuries like mattresses, the men just slept on their heavy topcoats. However the forepeak did have a cupboard where the tinned milk was stored and a 'monkey stove', a small coal burner, which kept them warm and was used for brewing the all-important tea. The cocklers liked their tea strong and sweet.

Mary Amelia was worked twelve months a year, seven days a week, whenever the weather was suitable. They could not go out in an easterly; they called it a 'starvation wind' because the banks they worked on became a dangerous lee shore. The winter time was the worst, out on the open sands, bent up, hand raking the cockles. It was particularly bad when the wind 'was up east' as it was unbelievably cold or as George put it 'was bloody cold, mate, and we pissed on our hands to keep them warm'.

The Leigh sailing cocklers had almost flat bottoms, to enable them to run on the sandbanks, and centreboards to drop down and grip the water so that they could sail against the wind. When afloat *Mary Amelia* looks like a bawley, but out of the water she appears to be the shape of a small barge for carrying shellfish.

The *Mary Amelia* used to load 365 bushels, probably over 4 tons of cockles, and if they could find enough cockles she floated with only the top plank amidships above the water. As soon as the boat 'fleeted' (floated) they hauled in the anchor and set off for the boiling sheds in the creek at Old Leigh. In a fresh breeze the lee deck was often under water and a cold spray drove across the boat. The men in the 'steerage' aft had nothing more than their topcoats to keep them warm and when they had sailed up the creek to the cockle sheds at Old Leigh, they still had several hours work to do. The cockles had to be put into baskets and carried ashore to the sheds on yokes for steaming.

We suggested to George Osborne that cockling must have been hard manual work, done under conditions which men from the computer-age society of western Europe would have found totally unacceptable. 'We were all the same, so we accepted it' said George. All the men living in the little narrow street of Old Leigh had been either a cockler or a fisherman on one of the bawleys. George told us that no cocklers were ever lost or men drowned, 'It was hard work, but it never killed any of us'. It certainly hadn't hurt George. He was nearly ninety when we met him, sitting in his room with photographs of the Osborne's *Mary Amelia* and their four cocklers called *Renown* on the walls. They had been independent men and he had absolutely loved the life.

Cockling might not have killed anyone, but white weeding certainly had killed one of *Mary Amelia's* owners. He had been knocked overboard by the mainsail and had drowned.

John Leather came to look at *Mary Amelia* one winter's day and told us about the motor cocklers he knew between 1948 and 1953. He had been on holiday at Leigh and greatly admired the smart new boats working from the creek. John remembers the Leigh men were much more 'cockney', than the Essex men from the rivers Blackwater and Colne. On the cocklers there was a lot of leg pulling and endless card games were played while motoring to and from the grounds. The Essex smackmen of the Colne and Blackwater, who had a tradition of spending the summer as paid crews on gentlemen's yachts, were much more reserved.

In January 2004, not long after we had met George Osborne, I joined Jonathan on a passage down the Essex coast. It was a reasonably calm day, although the flat-bottomed *Mary Amelia* bounced about a bit in the sea off Walton Naze. The cold weather was not the real problem. In modern weather proofed clothing we were actually warm, but with so many layers we moved around with the agility of men in moon suits. We had hoped to make Andy Harman's yard in one tide, but this meant going into Brightlingsea then up to the head of St Osyth Creek. Alan Williams, one of the independent shipwrights based at St Osyth Boatyard, was going to put a centreboard back in to *Mary Amelia*. Alan had worked on the Australian 120ft three masted tops'l schooner *Alma Doepel* which had two huge dagger boards, and when he came home he rebuilt the Severn trow *Spry*.

Because it was winter we had waited a long time to pick the right weather to go down the coast, in fact we had waited too long to make sure it was going to be a settled day, and left rather late on the tide. The delay meant that instead of having a favourable tide the whole way, the tide turned against us just after Walton Pier. We had a long way to go to reach Brightlingsea before dark.

After the tide turned progress was painfully slow, just three knots over the ground, and we knew it was going to be impossible to reach St Osyth Creek that day. By Jaywick the light was fading into a grey unwelcoming sky. Neither of us spoke, we were apprehensive about going into Brightlingsea in a winter fog. In the old days back in *Sea Fever* and *L'Atalanta* I would have been worrying about losing the landmarks to aid pilotage, but Jonathan has a wonderful satellite navigator which told us our exact position. The tiny arrow on the Sat Nav moved up the River Colne and we went alongside the pontoons at Brightlingsea. It was dark and cold and there was no one in sight on the water or ashore.

We went home for the night, believing that the difficult part of the passage was over, and planned to return the next day to make the short trip up to 'Toosey', as the locals call St Osyth. I was looking forward it, I took my camera, but when we returned to Brightlingsea next morning the wind was blowing hard. As the tide was not high enough for us to reach St Osyth, we repaired to the warmth of the fish and chip shop to fortify ourselves for the short easy trip. Well, that was the plan.

The *Mary Amelia* sailing past the Ramsholt "Arms"

When we came back to the foreshore the wind had risen into a south-west gale, blowing right up Brightlingsea Creek. On the water a cabin cruiser broke loose from her moorings and was blown up the creek at an amazing speed. In our tiny dinghy, one we carried on deck, Jonathan was unable to row against the wind and tide. We tried rowing together and finished up exhausted back against the Colne Yacht Club jetty. I went round to the Smack Dock and found Paul Winter and the owner of *Blackbird* who were checking to see that the smacks had not parted from their lines in the gale. Brian of the *Blackbird* offered to lend us an outboard, saying it was an old one and it didn't matter if it went to the bottom. In a cloud of spray, most of which went over me in the bow, we managed to get out to *Mary Amelia,* but actually our problems were only just beginning. It was extremely dangerous standing on pontoons in the full force of a gale with spray crashing over them. I got aboard *Mary Amelia* and started the engine, but there was so much strain on the mooring ropes that we had a real fight to get them off. I held the boat at full astern while Jonathan, on all fours, let the final rope go. By this time the ebb had already started, but the force of wind wanted to take us up on to Cindery Island. I went full ahead, weaving at speed between the moorings and shot up the creek, taking 'the first right' up St Osyth Creek, where it was peaceful. With the wind astern I was not sure if we would stop at the wharf at the creek head but willing hands were there to take our lines. There is a moral to this little adventure; with boats the easy trips can often turn out to be the most dangerous.

The slot cut in the bottom of the *Mary Amelia* for the centreboard.

Up in the yard Alan Williams began work and cut a slit with a chain saw, the mechanized adze, in *Mary Amelia's* keel. Cutting a hole in the bottom of a boat sounds like asking for trouble, so why do it? Clearly it was going to alter the already limited accommodation in the cabin. After all Jonathan's main reason for buying this 34ft boat was to replace the 22ft Great Yarmouth shrimper, *Crangon* that had a tiny cuddy forward only just big enough for us to lie down in to sleep.

Selling a boat is like losing a member of your family. My first boat *Sea Fever* vanished into the French canals and I never heard of her again. We thought it was going the same way with the *Crangon*. The last I saw of her was her lights shining in the darkness out on our mooring. By next morning the young German who had bought her had vanished into a stiff southwesterly, towards Ramsgate. He had promised to tell us when he reached Hamburg, but it was two years before he phoned to say that he had reached their destination safely after a three-week trip.

Two incidents tipped the scales in favour of the centreboard. The first was the 40th East Coast Old Gaffer's Race from Brightlingsea. I was the only person to have entered a boat in all these races and had been much involved with the OGA for many years. In 1963 we had set out to save the gaff rig from extinction and been surprised when the rig became trendy. We had succeeded. Happy days, but it became repetitive and I wanted to try something different.

There was a light breeze at the start of this race and we drifted down the River Colne with sails just filling, actually the ebb tide was also powering us along. We were amongst

Alan Williams supervising the lowering of the new three quarter ton centreboard into *Mary Amelia* at St Oysth, 2004.

a bunch of silent drifting boats over on the shallows near Mersea Island Flats. Steve Hall, the sail maker, elected to use the lead line to test the depth. Steve had once been a crew on Jim Lawrence's bawley *Helen & Violet*, that had been sailed with great skill and a lot of humour.

'Four fathoms,' shouted Steve, and then a very quiet voice whispered, 'actually it's two.'

'Two fathoms,' shouted Steve, his voice carrying across the water while he softly added for us, 'one and a half.'

The two men in the little gaffer beside us were clearly listening to Steve and looked surprised when their echo-sounder's alarm went off warning them of shallow water. One of them dived below to check if there had been a mistake.

The *Mary Amelia* leaving the River Blackwater at 8.5 knots, motor and sail, to be in time to have enough water to cross the Deben bar.

'One and a half,' cried Steve as if he was hailing a taxi and then to us, 'One!' Almost at once the 44ft Essex smack sailing just beside us suddenly reared up in the water as her keel struck the bottom. Her crew who had been lolling on the deck suddenly sprung to their feet as the smack heeled over sending the boom crashing over. We looked astern and heard a diesel engine start and the smack dragged herself off the shallows and sadly out of the race.

It would be good to report that we picked up a few places by this ruse, but it didn't end that way. Once out of the Colne the *Mary Amelia's* ability to tack to windward was so bad that we gave up and ran back up the river to Wivenhoe. Here Steve, in his home waters, became 'Essex man in his natural habitat.' In thigh boots Steve went across the mud to commandeer a boat and then he sculled us across the river to the "Anchor" for a drink.

Sailing 'back up' wind to dredge back slowly with the wind on *Mary Amelia,* 2004. The winning smack, *Kate,* can be seen going back sideways to get oysters from the bottom with hand hauled dredges

To keep alive the skills of working under sail the smacks take part in The Mersea Oyster Dredging Match that is held on the Common Ground off Mersea Island. The *Kate, Marigold, Mayflower* and *Helen & Violet* can be seen dredging, 2004.

Actually this unscheduled drink was more fun than yet another race, but on another occasion we seriously needed to go to windward. We were going across the Thames Estuary on a boiling hot day, just Jonathan and myself, under power, as there was very little wind. It seemed like an easy trip. 'Pride before a fall' is probably the best way to describe it.

The tricky part of the trip was crossing the big ship channel, we waited our time and slipped in astern of a huge grey merchant vessel thundering up to the Port of London, very much aware that there was another vessel just visible on the horizon. Then the engine stopped dead, it is air cooled and had overheated. We were a sitting duck in the big ship channel.

Even when we were racing things on *Mary Amelia* had tended to get done at a relaxed speed, but on this occasion Jonathan worked like a madman on his own to 'set the gear.' Up went the whole lot, tops'l and even the jib tops'l made one of its rare appearances.

Fortunately a typical late afternoon land breeze came wafting down the estuary and we started clapping along at a fine speed, heading at 5 knots straight for the Middle Sand. I put the tiller down to come about; but because the hull was not gripping the water nothing happened, she just kept going straight. Jonathan climbed on the tiny foredeck of the heeling boat to reduce sail. We both knew, but didn't say, that if he slipped overboard I would not have been able to tack back and get him.

There is a shallow channel over the Middle Sands and the *Mary Amelia* must have been here before, as she sailed straight though this channel. We had been heading for the first of Bill Colman's Whitstable Oyster Dredging Matches and in the haze saw two smacks, the *Stormy Petrel* and the *Thistle,* beating slowly along the shore of the Isle of Sheppey. It cheered us up not to be alone, but it was dangerous to have a boat which couldn't be tacked at sea.

The cocklers from Leigh Creek were one of the few sailing British workboats to have centreboards. Barges overcame the problems of sailing in the shallow estuaries and creeks by using leeboards, but by the 1890s this line of development had reached as far as it could go. Heyward at Southend and a few other builders had fitted centreboards, but this phase had only lasted a few years until engines were introduced.

When an engine was fitted in *Mary Amelia* the centreboard was cut out. In 1980, *Mary Amelia* had been a hulk sunk on the foreshore of the River Orwell at Trimley. Many old workboats in this state don't get past November 5, but *Mary Amelia* would probably have rotted away if Colin Fox had not decided to rebuild her. First the hull had to be refloated and towed up river to Pin Mill. By the time they reached Hare's Creek, just down river from Pin Mill, things were going very badly and the old cockler was filling with water. She was towed over into the shallows where she went 'down like a submarine,' according to Colin Fox, who had stood on the wheelhouse roof in his thigh boots until Mick Lungley had come over in the launch to pick him up. Several years later we went to the party in Fred Webb's shed to celebrate the rebuilding of *Mary Amelia*.

Before Alan Williams fitted the centreboard he wanted to look at an original cockler's centreboard case, but the nearest we could get to the original were traces of one in the 1904 cockler *Alice & Florrie*. She had been sheeted in ferro-cement, not everybody's idea of the best way to preserve a wooden hull, but all the fabric of the original hull had survived inside. A visit to *Alice & Florrie* in Alresford Creek one bright day in February revealed the size and method of fitting her centreboard.

The original Leigh cocklers had been called 'galleys', which was the old Thames Estuary term for sizable open boats. The later sailing cocklers were decked, but the thwarts (seats), going across the hull were kept to give strength when loaded with cockles.

Alan Williams worked on fitting the new centreboard case and strengthening the thwarts, and we fitted out the *Mary Amelia* at the weekends. She was actually right outside Andy and Jane Harman's front door, and as we painted, in the spring sunshine, their young daughter and her friends played around nearby.

Dick Harman with the stowboating smack *Ellen* at the St Osyth Boatyard.

On his way to the back door, Dick Harman, Andy's father, who had restored the smack *ADC* in 1968, used to stop to have a chat and seemed to be watching our progress with interest. Looking at *Mary Amelia* Dick announced, 'You couldn't have a better boat for about here. You can get up any creek, lay on the cant edge for the night and if you've got a dog, just let it run ashore.'

Sara, stuck in the mud while Harry has made it to hulk of the Brightlingsea scalloping smack *William & Eliza.* In the background is James & Stone's old shipyard, on Brightlingsea waterside, shortly before it was pulled down for housing, 2004.

Dick had a soft spot for *Mary Amelia* because he had once worked the 42ft tripper boat *Nemo II* off Clacton beach. This tripper boat had also been built by Heyward with almost the same shaped hull. Once he had been chartered for the grand opening of the Colchester Oyster Fishery in Pyefleet. For this the Mayor of Colchester and the clerk turn out in their full regalia, an ancient custom full of colour. Being almost flat-bottomed the *Nemo II* went into shallow water where the prop picked up a bottle that went straight through the bottom of the boat.

The mayor and his party were quite game to swim for it, but they had the priceless town mace with them and were greatly worried it would finish up on the bottom of the River Colne. Fortunately the *Nemo II* had bulkheads and she arrived back at Brightlingsea safely, but the water was nearly up to the deck level. The Colchester Town Mace did not get wet and the dignity of the mayor's party had remained intact.

Boatyards are not just places where boats are returned to good health, they are part of the social fabric of the coastal life. Tea break at the St Osyth yard was a great social event. In the weekdays the shipwrights bonded over a cup of tea, while at the weekend the boat owners continued the ritual. The cheerful group sat on some old chairs under the counter stern of a yacht and discussed the morning's problems and gave opinions on world affairs.

St Osyth Boatyard is a well-organized jumble of boats, mostly wooden, with the 80ft sailing barge *Edme* taking the central berth. A syndicate from the yard owns *Edme* with Andy as skipper and the driving force. By the end of *Mary Amelia's* stay the yard had been emptied of all the boats that were going out that season and *Edme* had slipped away for a weekend to train up her crew for another season of barge racing.

The St Osyth barge *Edme* running up the River Orwell to win the Pin Mill Barge Match. 2004.

The Edme had been built for Richard Horlock, by Canns, at Harwich in 1898 and been named after the Edme Maltings at Mistley. Over a century later the Edme Maltings were still in production and the *Edme* was still sailing. Andy hit on the idea of carrying a freight of their produce. The result, in 2002, was a token cargo of Edme's Food Ingredients, flaked wheat, from Mistley to Green's Mill at Maldon. As the *Edme* does not have an engine the voyage was as authentic as one made by a commercial sailing barge. Keen to reach the welcoming party at Maldon the *Edme* put out from Harwich into the tail end of a force 6 south westerly. She is a very good sailing barge, but was unable to beat around Walton Naze. They ran back into Harwich for shelter and two days later the *Edme* put to sea again. By the time she came ghosting past Osea Island it was the other extreme, the wind had faded away, and she was towed up to Maldon by Rick Cardy's tug *GW 108*.

Andy Harman with a coil of rope on the barge *Edme* passing the coastal vessels *Locator*, and *Roan* before going alongside Green's Mill, Maldon, 2002.

View across the twisting channel of the River Alde to the Blackheath Mansion.

In St Osyth Creek the *Edme* is towed by the yard's work boat, this is just to save time as Andy and his loyal crew can do it all under sail. They have, after all, visited the most difficult place on the East Coast to reach under sail. In 1990 George Gooderham offered a prize for the first barge to get up to Snape under sail only.

Snape, at the head of the River Alde was reckoned, by the old bargemen, to be the most difficult place to reach on the East Coast. The bargemen used to say that 'the Suffolk Rivers were nothing more than big old creeks.' I suppose that must make Snape, with a lonely quay sitting at the head of several miles of mud flats, the ultimate creek port. In one reach, above Iken Cliff, the channel goes right round to point back down river towards the sea, but the most difficult part is in the final reaches below Snape Maltings where the river is narrow and shallow.

A bargeman from Sittingbourne once told me that he had taken a week to go, from Iken Church to Snape Maltings, in a sailing barge loaded with bricks. With the help of the hufflers they had kedged up a little distance at the top of each high tide. It would not have taken long to walk along the river wall. The *Beatrice Maud's* barley freight in 1939 was the last time that a barge had been to the Maltings under sail until the *Edme* arrived to claim the prize in 1994

History in the mud. Phil Harding of "Time Team" in St. Osyth's Creek.

Chapter Eight

Navigation by Instinct

All the work on the *Mary Amelia's* centreboard stopped when the Channel 4 'Time Team' arrived to investigate Alan Williams' theory that there was a medieval quay in St Osyth Creek, just down from the Harman's yard. Further down the creek was an old farm dock where the remains of the stackie barge *Bluebell* were just visible. She had been, with the little *Cygnet*, the last of the farm barges that carried stack freights from the River Stour right up until 1939. 'Time Team' were not interested in nineteenth century barge wharves, but they hoped to find something linking the area with St Osyth Priory and the creek's Saxon past.

Tony Robinson tasting sea salt from the boiling pans during the making of the 'Time Team' programme at St Osyth.

St Osyth was the daughter of a King of East Anglia who, in an arranged marriage, was given to the King of the East Saxons. St Osyth had not been keen on the idea of marriage and during the wedding feast, shortly before she was due to lose her virginity, she ran off to join a nunnery. The king seems to have been equally glad to get rid of his troublesome bride and gave her the village, which bears her name, where she established her own nunnery.

St Osyth's luck ran out when the Danish Vikings raided this part of the coast. They caught St Osyth and cut off her head, reputedly in the wood overlooking the creek. The account recorded later said that before she actually died, she picked up her head and carried it to the church door. Where she fell a spring appeared and the water from this spring had the power to work miracles. The medieval church thrived on such legends.

In 1121 a new Priory in her name was established on the hilltop, but 'Time Team' wanted to establish a link between the old quay in the creek and the village that grew up around the Priory. At low tide in the bottom of the creek the 'Time Team' excavated the quay where the stone from St Osyth Priory was probably shipped out when this monastic establishment was pulled down after Henry VIII closed down all the monastic establishments.

The 'Time Team' artist Victor Ambrus pondering on ways to portray the Tudor wharf being excavating by Gus Milne and Alan Williams in St Osyth Creek, 2004.

We left St Osyth early one May morning, and only a few people witnessed our departure. Once out into the River Colne we spotted Gerrard Swift coming to meet us towing the *Musset* over the Mersea Flats. Gerrard, a barge skipper who also repairs traditional wooden boats, had stopped the leaks in the *Musset* by putting three new planks in our smack's boat. With *Musset* fastened astern we headed for the Deben and once out into the open Wallet, up went the sails and then the big moment, Jonathan lowered the centreboard. Standing at the tiller I saw the bow suddenly come up into the wind. The *Mary Amelia*, with her restored 7ft draft, gripped the water and no longer made dramatic leeway. When we tried tacking through the wind, the bow slowly paid off on the new tack. The expense and trouble had been worthwhile.

Because all the men who understood centreboards in Leigh cocklers have long gone, the knowledge of them is as remote as the sail plan of an Anglo-Saxon longship. Later in the summer we found a design fault with the new centreboard. It was a case of pride before a fall. At the start of East Coast Old Gaffer's Race off Brightlingsea a mass of gaff boats jockeyed for position, and when we turned to reach up the River Blackwater with the centreboard down, the *Mary Amelia* surprised us by suddenly starting to move up the fleet at speed. We thought we would save a tack by hauling it up and go over the shallow ground off Bradwell. A brilliant plan if it had worked, but the centreboard just touched the ground and wouldn't come up. We heaved again on the centreboard winch, but the block broke, leaving the plate down.

We sailed back into Brightlingsea and the crew left. On the mobile it was fixed up for a diver to come and shackle a new block on to the top of the centreboard. The next evening the diver, Shaun O'Dell, arrived at slack water for a twenty-minute job. However we had been the talk of Brightlingsea waterfront and word had reached the ear of the Harbour Master. When Jonathan met him ashore he was told that there was a ban on single divers within the Harbour area.

Brightlingsea was still very active as a creek port, every year eighty ships of around 2,500-tonnes take scrap iron from Brightlingsea Wharf to Spain, while twenty barges a month leave with ballast for London. Brightlingsea did not want any trouble with 'health and safety' issues. As one local man put it 'years ago when this place was just fishing boats and yachts we had a harbour master, but at least he went home at five o'clock.'

We had planned to go over to Pyefleet to retrieve the centreboard, but the night before Jim Lawrence had come down to the bar of the Colne Yacht Club and given us better advice. Jim had sailed on the River Colne for decades, starting as a skipper of sailing barges in the 1950s and after that he became a renowned sail maker at Brightlingsea. He suggested we went over to East Mersea Stone, a shingle point in the River Colne. Here, at low water we would find still clear water at slack tide.

The next morning at 4am we woke to a fine day and the tide high enough to get out of the creek and over to Mersea Stone. The early morning sunlight lit up the shingle point and locals walking their dogs waved cheerfully to the black cockler anchored really close to the shore. At 8am, as planned, John Brett ferried out the still cheerful Shaun O'Dell and he quickly solved the problem. Jonathan hauled on the winch, up came the centreboard and we went forward, hauled up the anchor and headed home for the Deben. We had made this trip so many times that we did not need to look at the charts.

Human beings, unlike many species of birds and animals, can't find their way to distant destinations by instinct, but if they spend a lifetime in one place they can develop a kind of sixth sense. Some of the sailing smack skippers owned charts, but they were expensive items so were often left at home. Besides it was a matter of pride not to rely on them.

Back at St Osyth Dick Harman had talked about his early days in the Brightlingsea smacks that had not carried charts or tide tables, the fishermen had found their way around the narrow channels in the Thames Estuary without them. The old skippers had spent their whole lives in the Thames Estuary fishery and had few outside interests so that their whole intelligence had been devoted to these waters. This allowed them to develop an extraordinary ability to navigate. The skippers knew the compass courses off by heart and, apart from the Wallet Spitway buoy, which was essential for finding their way over the channel at the Gunfleet Sands, they did not bother much with navigation buoys. Their main use for navigation buoys was to see which way the tide was flowing. The skippers watched the surface to gauge the depth of the water from the way the tide made the surface behave. In foggy weather they followed along the edge of the sandbanks watching for seaweed and debris floating in the slack water.

Dick had joined the Brightlingsea smack *Charlotte Ellen,* skippered by Dennis Heard, in 1951 for one of the last seasons of the ancient 'stowboating' for sprat. That season the shoals were all over on the Kent shore and the *Charlotte Ellen* had worked from The Swale and returned to land her catch at the canning factory at Wivenhoe. Money was short when only a few fish were caught and the *Charlotte Ellen's* crew used to go around the pubs with a bucket of sprat to raise enough cash to buy bread.

The bargemen, who made far longer passages than the smacks, also tended to do their navigation in their heads. They memorized the compass course from buoy to buoy. They knew the speed that they were travelling 'over the ground' and with the help of an old Woolworth's alarm clock could, in fog or haze, time their progress from buoy to buoy.

The longest passage I have taken part in where 'all in your head' navigation, was used was in 1973 when we came back from Holland on the barge *Redoubtable.* When we came out of Ostende the barge's owner George Gooderham, an offshore yachtsman, gave the skipper Headley Farrington, a compass course to steer for Ramsgate. Headley, actually a rather pleasant old man, took this as a personal affront to his professional standing and refused to take any notice of this course, saying, with considerable condescension, 'I can't trust any of you boys!'

Headley had been one of the top Colchester skippers and had 'gone ashore' to be the manager of the barge firm of Francis & Gilders for about twenty years. By this time he was well into his seventies, but had never been across the 'other side' of the North Sea before. We 'boys' actually had already sailed across the North Sea.

Headley stayed at the wheel all day, and would not allow anyone else to steer, although he had nipped below a few times to look at the chart, locking the wheel before he left the deck. The owner continued his navigation checks and things came to a head in late afternoon when yellow streaks in the water confirmed his suspicions that we were somewhere on top of the Goodwin sands. Reluctantly Headley was obliged to follow the owner's orders and head back to deep water. When we arrived at Ramsgate in the evening the skipper was clearly a very tired man and made a complete mess of coming alongside.

Next morning we were off again and Headley was very happy to be back in his home waters, telling us the route he would be taking. We had guessed he was steering from buoy to buoy on courses he remembered from his days as skipper, decades before. By the time we were off Margate our skipper was a very worried man, pacing about on the deck quietly muttering oaths. Trinity House had moved the buoys slightly so that they kept popping up in unexpected positions. Going up the Swin to the Spitway even more of the buoys had been moved, but the channel is narrow in places and Headley was clearly watching out for discolouration of water to tell him where the banks were. Finally off Harwich fog came down and Headley had no answer for this, we could hear the big ships in the channel just ahead of us. He did the seaman-like thing, shouted for the anchor to be let go, coming forward to make sure we threw the chain over the windlass correctly.

Headley's refusal to take any notice of a course from a chart was very irritating, both George and myself could have made the passage a lot easier for him. However the able old barge master felt he could, had the situation demanded, have made the whole passage from the River Schelde to Harwich without any charts. After all the men he first went to sea with had done just that.

Men were making voyages around the North Sea long before compasses were introduced, fixing their position from where the sun was in the sky and their knowledge of the behaviour and depth of the sea. Long waves in deep water, steep waves in shallow water. They also, no doubt when they sat around their fires, talked about what to look for on a coastal passage and then memorised these 'sailing directions.'

There is plenty of evidence from Roman writers that the peoples of northern Europe were crossing the North Sea to raid and trade with the British Isles. They appear to have been using boats with sails and they don't seem to have had too much trouble finding their destinations. It is possible that one raiding party, from one of the Frankish or Saxon tribes, crossed the North Sea and went far inland up the River Ouse to burn, and no doubt loot, Godmanchester.

We have some idea of the type of ship that might have been used for these voyages because in 1939 the shape of one was found in Mound One at Sutton Hoo. Basil Brown, the local archaeologist who made the initial discovery, carefully traced out the shape of the huge 89ft longship in the sandy soil. They found the burial chamber in the centre of the hull and there was tremendous excitement when the royal treasure was excavated.

The Sutton Hoo excavation was done at speed because the situation with Nazi Germany was deteriorating fast; World War II started within a few weeks of the treasure being taken out of the Sutton Hoo ship. Unfortunately the ship itself was not seen as a priority, but a team led by Lieutenant-Commander J.K.D. Hutchison made drawings and detailed notes. Tragically Hutchison was killed during the war and his flat was bombed so that the drawings of the hull were lost forever.

An intriguing question about the Sutton Hoo ship was whether it had carried a sail. Hutchison's plan might have helped with details, but photographs show that when the treasure chamber was excavated in 1939 the soil under it had been disturbed. Every one was so excited by the treasure that they did not record whether there had been a mast case, there was no sign of a side rudder either, but the stern did have extra frames, presumably to take the weight of one.

After the excavation in 1939 some experts claimed, because she did not have a deep keel, the Sutton Hoo longship could not have been a sailing sea going craft. They over looked the fact that there had been many small working craft, with shoal draft to operate

Angela Evans at the British Museum showing members of the Sutton Hoo Society part of the golden treasure found in the Anglo-Saxon ship burial in 1939

in shallow waters, used both sail and oar. The Suffolk inshore fishing boats, like my *Three Sisters,* were often rowed against the wind. Until engines arrived no one thought it unusual to row a boat at sea against the wind. As the Sutton Hoo longship drew very little water she would have been ideal for going up creeks.

It was the promise of building a replica that led me to become involved with the Sutton Hoo Society. In 1989, as chairman, I tried to get the ball rolling to actually build a replica so that we could relearn the secrets of the past. I read that a small replica of a Saxon longship was going to be at the traditional boat rally at Henley-on-Thames. Sure enough there was a small replica of the Anglo-Saxon ship, a cargo carrying craft that had been found on the Kent marshes, in a drainage ditch at Graveney.

Under a single square sail the replica ship *Ottor* was being happily tacked up and down the Thames sailed by its owners, Edwin and Joyce Gifford, a retired couple from the New Forest, who had approached the subject of early sailing craft with a missionary zeal. While sailing up the Thames at Henley on the *Ottor* with the Giffords I asked if they had thought of building a replica of the Sutton Hoo ship. The Giffords were delighted that someone from Sutton Hoo was interested in their project and went on to build the half-length replica of the Sutton Hoo longship.

Sam Newton came up with the name *Sae Wylfing,* Anglo Saxon for 'the Sea Wolf's cub'. During the trials the long narrow hull of the 44ft *Sae Wylfing* proved fast running with the wind with her single square sail, and very fast reaching across the wind. She sometimes has to be rowed around when tacking against the wind but gibing is easier. She can make progress against the wind, although by modern expectations this is slow.

With *Sae Wylfing* Edwin and Joyce and their loyal crew from CHES (Colchester Re-enactment Society) have shown that the Anglo-Saxon long ships, as well as being

The *Sae Wylfing* sailing with one reef down near the Horse Sand, River Deben, 2004.

Edwin Gifford getting ready to sail the *Sae Wylfing* at Ramsholt Dock, 2004.

The wharf at Fordwich on the Great Stour River is now deep in the countryside of Kent, but once, when the Wantsum was tidal, it was the port for Canterbury.

Tom Burnham, left, on his Deal beach boat *Lady Irene* going down the River Stour below Sandwich, 2002.

rowed, were undoubtedly capable of sailing. Their studies and passion for the early ships has made them leading experts in Anglo-Saxon ships, but after fifteen years of *Sae Wylfing* being sailed there are still lessons to be learnt.

The original 89ft Sutton Hoo ship would have been ideal for voyages across the Thames Estuary to Kent. Her shallow draft would have allowed her to pass over many shoals and banks and on arrival her long lean bow would have extended up the beach so that the crew could have jumped ashore without getting too wet.

Under sail and oar she could have made a long coastal passage to Kent in a day. It is assumed that Raedwald, King of East Anglia, went by sea to meet his ally, the King of Kent, in a Great Hall at Canterbury. The most likely landing was Fordwich, a large village just to the east of Canterbury. This is at the navigable head of the Great Stour River. The modern Fordwich is deep in the Kent countryside, but in the Anglo-Saxon period it was a totally different place. Fordwich was then on a small estuary of the River Stour leading down to the Wantsum, a wide tidal channel linking Pegwell Bay with the Thames behind the Isle of Thanet. Since the Anglo-Saxon period the Wantsum has completely silted up and turned into grazing marshes.

Assuming Raedwald, King of East Anglia, who is believed to have been buried in the Sutton Hoo ship, crossed the Thames Estuary in his ship in a day, he would then have gone east along the north Kent coast down to the Roman fort at the Reculver and then turned south into the Wantsum. After five miles in the Wantsum the ship would have turned west up the Great Stour River and arrived at Fordwich.

In a smooth sea and fair wind the Sutton Hoo ship could have exceeded 10 knots. If the weather turned against her, which would have been the norm, an alternative route to

Members of the Sutton Hoo Society dressed as King Raedwald of East Anglia. These costumes are replicas of the regalia found in Mound One at Sutton Hoo in 1939.

Canterbury could have been to land in the Swale near Graveney, where there is evidence of some form of a Saxon settlement, and go on by land. If there had been a head wind it is doubtful if the Sutton Hoo ship could have been rowed at much more than 3 knots, and to keep this up for a long period the oarsmen would probably have rowed in two watches.

The Anglo-Saxon shipmasters might have set out just before dawn, when the sky was already getting light, and would have tried to make most of the coastal passage before sunset. In a clear moonlit night they could have picked out the landmarks, but in the dark a low coast and offshore banks are very hard to spot until you are almost on to them. Presumably when faced with adverse conditions the Saxons would have run their craft up on the shore and camped, sometimes spending days sitting around the campfire watching the sky to try and foretell when it was safe to sail on.

By the time the Sutton Hoo Ship was built early in the 7th century the Saxons had been roaming around the North Sea for at least two hundred years so they would have worked out where to keep the sun's position in the sky to steer a course in the open sea. The pilotage information would have been passed down amongst the men who steered the ships and they would have had names to describe every river and bank. They probably had rhymes to help them remember the course to steer.

From north Kent the Saxon mariner could have gone through the Wantsum and then across the Straits of Dover to the French coast, this must have been a very old route even then, and from here they would have turned north to go to the mouth of the River Schelde and the European trading centres. A voyage to the old homelands in northern Germany might have been done in three weeks, but in a bad summer it might have lasted a couple of months. However a shipmaster skilled enough to find his way across the open sea might have taken three or four days between East Anglia and River Elbe. Being caught in a gale in an open boat would have been wet and totally exhausting for the crew, there would have been nowhere to shelter from the weather and they would have had to bail continually. An open boat can, providing it runs with the seas, survive in a moderate gale, but a severe gale with breaking wave tops would have swamped them. All sailors dread being caught on a lee shore but the Saxons could land through surf.

The Saxons also made long voyages around the British coast and another likely voyage for King Raedwald of East Anglia was to meet the King of Northumberland in North of the Humber Lands. It would certainly, in the good summer weather, have been quicker and safer to sail up the coast than go by horse. In the Anglo-Saxon period there was a small harbour, now filled in by sand, just north of Bamburgh Castle, and the Sutton Hoo ship could have voyaged here.

The actual conditions at sea haven't changed. Often the impoverished coastal communities went on using the simple forms of pilotage used by the early navigators. The main improvement was the compass but in their home waters men could often find their way around without charts.

The boats didn't change much either. The legacy of the open clinker Anglo-Saxon ships lasted into the twentieth century. The last working examples of the double-enders are the open, wooden, clinker boats used off the north Norfolk coast for crabbing. The fishermen kept them, until high-speed plastic craft were available and advertised in *Fishing News*, because their beamy hulls were ideal for riding through the surf in the shallow water close to the beach and their pointed sterns broke the waves rolling up behind them. A useful tool will remain in use until a better one is devised.

Chapter Nine

A Shopping Breeze

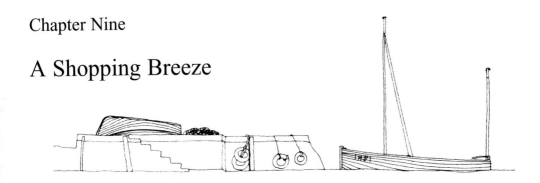

Our cottage has enjoyed modest local fame for its small orchard of plum trees, but we lived there for forty-five years before I got around to trying to identify the variety of the remaining trees. We took a branch into Notcutt's Nursery and at the Advice Centre they identified them as Oullin's Golden Gage. The plum trees appear to be over a century old, but we have no way of telling who planted them. Plum trees are part of the character of the place, a character fixed by some unknown person in the past. In our time we have updated the cottage and clearly previous generations did the same.

We used to sail up to Waldringfield in the *Pet,* on shopping expeditions, and from the Deben it looks like the kind of place where 'time has stood still,' but each generation has

changed it. In the Victorian period the River Deben was very much the commercial highway and the hard landing beach at Waldringfield gave employment. Sailing barges came onto the beach and the Church charged them to berth here to load straw and hay for London. The same barges came back with muck and when this was carted up through the street everyone closed their doors and windows against the stench. Dust and smoke were added to the atmosphere when in 1872 a cement factory was started here, and there was also a coprolite washing plant in the break in the cliff.

At Waldringfield, the landlord of the 'Maybush', Isaac Stollery, organised the barge freights and when several barges were loaded the workers often slept the night on the pub floor. Stollery also ran a ferry across to Sutton and this appears to have continued after his death until 1908 when the cement factory closed.

The 'Maybush' at Waldringfield on an early August morning, 2004.

Barges, with their lofty masts and rusty red sails, will dominate any waterside area. The stackie trade on the Deben petered out during World War I, but by then the first pleasure boaters were arriving. With the barge traffic dying the river was virtually empty. There were very few yachts and the ancient oaks hung over its undamaged shore. The early boating people must have thought they had found paradise.

The increase in leisure boating turned Waldringfield into an entirely different place. The first village regatta had been held in 1906, but in 1921 eleven enthusiasts met in a beach hut at Waldringfield and decided to form a sailing club. Soon a stream of recruits arrived by small car and bicycle. When the regatta was first held two extra buses were put on to bring people out from Ipswich. The old cement quay became a boatyard; Mr Stollery built some of the first beach huts, rather grandly called bungalows. The village became an orderly residential community and Waldringfield Sailing Club grew into a well-organized family club with many members being second or third generation. There are rubbish bins carefully labelled stating what visitors can leave, if anyone unloaded a barge of muck on Waldringfield beach the entire population would be writing angry letters to the Council for months.

In the autumn when we sailed up to Waldringfield to go shopping, the river was often deserted and providing we kept still as we sailed passed Hemley Point, the huge flocks of gulls and waders took no notice of us. Sometimes a seal would pop its head out of the water to reconnoitre and then return to its underwater fish hunting.

The Waldringfield shop was up the narrow village street that leads away from the beach. Once we arrived during their dinner hour but they heard us talking and they came out and kindly opened the shop for us. All this stopped when Tesco opened a superstore a few miles away on this side of Ipswich.

The Waldringfield Sailing Club's 14ft Dragonfly class, racing during the revival weekend, 2004.

The Tide Mill quay, Woodbridge and the new restaurant at the Granary, 2004.

After the Waldringfield shop closed we started going up river to Woodbridge. The same routine, but because the Deben dries out it meant we could not leave until half flood tide. When the *Three Sisters* powerful fore lug and mizzen are hoisted she is off up river like a terrier after a rat. The fore lug is not far removed from the square sail of the medieval ships.

In the days when Frank Knights presided over his Woodbridge boat yard we used to drop in and tie up in the jumble of boats banging about on the Ferry Steps. But Woodbridge waterside has changed and we must do the same. In 2003 a smart new quay 'for visitors' was built, with some cash from the Lottery, near the Tide Mill. We touch in here, go in for a meal and forget to go up to the shops in the town.

Most of the East Coast boating centres now have some form of Eating Place, seven sprung up around the Ipswich Wet Dock when the yachts arrived, but it didn't used to be like that. When I first went 'messing about in boats' on the East Coast in the 1950s we just sailed from pub to pub. The only sustenance on offer would be packets of potato crisps or nuts. A pub which offered more than one flavour of crisps was ahead of the pack. In those days 'tourism' was only just starting to make an impact on the coast and most pubs remained 'working men club's', dark rooms with wooden benches and scrubbed tiled floors and no pretensions to comfort. All these pubs still had the tremendous character of nineteenth century Suffolk and the presence of the Landlord was always felt. Since then pubs have become run by 'restaurant managers' and often the Landlord is nowhere to be seen. In the old days he or she was always there to greet you. People went in to chat to their favourite Landlord.

At Waldringfield, the 'Maybush,' had one of the most colourful landlords in Albert Hill, a big man who often wore a trilby hat pulled down over one eye, even in the bar. No one messed with Albert, he had great strength of character and everyone behaved in his pub, but most people begrudgingly liked him. Albert used to lean over the bar as if he was about to tell you his deepest secrets, and part with one of his wide range of funny stories.

Albert's father had been a farmer in the village and once found corn kept going missing from his barn. Being a down to earth man Mr Hill senior put a rat trap on the inside of the little hole in the door where you push your finger through to open the latch. There were cries of pain as some unfortunate labourer, in search of free food for his chickens, had got his finger crushed, and this ended the problem of the missing grain. When Albert found things were going missing from his back shed he announced that he would be buying a rat trap. Everyone knew what he meant; nothing went missing from the shed again. There are people in Waldringfield, even now, who think twice before putting their finger in the hole of a latch.

Another popular Landlord was Sid Harper of the 'Jolly Sailor' at Orford, a totally different man. Again this pub was always run well, but it was done with a quiet charm. Mr Harper did not have any stories to tell passing sailors, but they were always made to feel welcome, although the regulars totally ignored occasional visitors. Just inside the door, as you stepped down, was a huge scrubbed wooden table with an everlasting game of dominoes going on. Big men in cloth caps fought out silent battles of wit on a daily basis in the 'Jolly Sailor.'

In any of these riverside pubs reaching the bar to get a drink required careful navigation, because there were usually local watermen watching your progress. Most of them had their own pint mugs which were invariably empty and you felt duty bound to buy them a drink. Even if you were not lying on one of their moorings, it was a wise precaution to have them on your side.

There were very few moorings at that time and in theory anyone could put down a mooring where they liked, but in practice it did not always work that way. The rivers were divided, unofficially, into the fiefdoms of watermen. If anyone laid a mooring without getting approval from them, at best the mooring simply vanished, or the boat mysteriously went adrift in bad weather. It was well worth buying that drink or, better still, discretely parting with a few crumpled notes. Once accepted by the local watermen they were your friends for life. Those who did not reach this status simply went off and took up golf.

There was a code of honour between watermen not to intrude into other people's areas. Once one of the Newsons, who were the pilots over the Deben bar, was delivering a large motor cruiser and because of bad weather decided to leave it anchored off Ramsholt Dock. Over the next few days the motor cruiser dragged its anchor all over the place and several boat owners wanted it moved. There were three watermen at Ramsholt and none of them one would touch the cruiser because 'if the Newsons had anchored it there, then it is perfectly alright.'

One of these watermen was old George Cook. His father had once gone, in the 1880s, as crew on a smack race in Walton on the Naze Regatta, but George worked on a farm. Since he lived near the water George helped out with the moorings, but his skills were limited to growing vegetables in his garden and then going across Ramsholt Ferry with a wheelbarrow and taking them several miles to sell them in Ipswich. Once the *Genesta* got into difficulties out in the river and they hailed Cookie for assistance. Unfortunately he was still wearing the farm hobnail boots and they left a lasting impression on the teak deck, before he fell through a skylight. The yacht owner thought it was better to give him a tip so that he would go back ashore.

While the sailors of the past have left a legacy of pubs at every landing, the idea of getting a meal ashore did not start to take shape until the mid-twentieth century. At Felixstowe Ferry we used to trudge up to the 'Ferry Boat' or 'Victoria', but after it opened in 1955 we increasingly stopped at the new 'Ferry Café'. This American prefabricated house, bought in Lincolnshire by Spencer Howlett for £130, was put up on the shingle just near the ferry landing. 'Shack city' was the name the locals called this hotchpotch of wooden sheds that grew up on a shingle spit.

Ever since Victorian times people had been going out to attractive riverside places, in the 1930s the 'Ramsholt Arms' did a nice line in afternoon teas, but Felixstowe Ferry remained a fishing hamlet so that a riverside café was something different here. However the 'Ferry Café' did not rely on tourism to start with, the café's main trade was fried breakfasts, when it opened at 6.45am, for the fishermen. It was busy again in the evening when the airman gathered, before getting the ferry back across the river to RAF Bawdsey. The 'Ferry Café' was never beautiful, but it has great functional character. We used to anchor *Sea Fever* inside the Horse Sand and go up to the Café for hot food. I liked it better than the pubs, there was always a seat and you did not have to buy anyone a drink.

Woodbridge riverside has changed a little from the days when we sailed up there in *Sea Fever*. The jumble of buildings, mostly boatyards, gave the place its charm of a working waterfront. Even when the boatyards were all active, with Robertsons, Whisstocks, Knights, Eversons and a few other shipwrights, it was still a fairly relaxed and quiet place. Then came the term 'redundant boatyard' and the property vultures began buying up these areas and trying for planning permission for housing.

Alan Crawford working at the Fisherman's Hut, Felixstowe Ferry. 2004

The same pattern of events had hit all the other waterside places on the East Coast, but they had reacted to it in different ways. At Burnham-on-Crouch one yacht yard was pulled down and replaced with housing and there have been developments on a larger scale along the River Colne at Wivenhoe and Rowhedge. At Ipswich Dock a new upmarket residential area rose up to tower above the old barge quays. Down river at Pin Mill new residents moved into the waterside hamlet and declared war on Webb's barge and yacht repair yard. Barges had been repaired there since the 1850s, but that did not stop new residents from campaigning to get it stopped. At the head of the River Blackwater some former mills were converted into flats, but the Green's flourmill just up river continued on. Only one motor barge, the *Locator,* regularly came up with freights of wheat. Some the new flat owners were protesting about the noise the barge made turning around and wanted it stopped. Expensive housing and working environments simply don't mix. Once houses arrive the residents campaign to get rid of maritime activities.

Each generation demands something different from a waterside place. In our Parish farm workers and watermen have been replaced with people 'down for the weekend' or working in Ipswich. The Suffolk villages are now very stimulating places, full of lively people, but it is very different from former times when people understood the farms and countryside around them.

When Linda Gould came to our Parish she quite misunderstood what was meant by 'the Shoot meets outside your house.' Coming from a background in fashion, she was delighted and expected a trendy photographer and glamorous models. Instead several shiny

Every year something new happens on the River Deben and in 2004 it was a, Waldringfield based, ice cream boat.

Woodbridge Riverside 2004, with the Ferry Dock, Frank Knights Yard, the former Whisstock Yard and the Tide Mill.

Land Rovers turned up, full of hearty men in plus fours armed with shotguns. This had been shoot to kill, not to impress.

As our family had grown up in Suffolk villages we considered our isolated rural life at The Cottage quite normal. To be honest as we had a car and telephone we were never cut off from the outside world in the way the old people were.

We had moved away from open coal fires but decided to fit a wood burner. Most of our friends in similar cottages had fitted wood burners about twenty years before, when they first became fashionable. The truth was when we were tenants we didn't like spending the money on someone else's property. When we became the owners one of the first things we wanted to do was put a wood burner in the living room, but it was still nine years before we took the plunge. While in Cornwall a Chinese stove was purchased at Trago Mills and brought back to Suffolk.

When the Alderton builder James Green arrived to fit the stove we embarked on a piece of property archaeology. We had been told by a young man from English Heritage that The Cottage dated from around 1620, with an eighteenth century piece added on to the east end, so we knew there was a good chance that the original open fireplace would be in there somewhere. While the dust was flying we went out shopping.

When we returned James said, 'I don't like being down here on my own, I heard voices'. It could have been someone shouting on the public footpath along the river wall. I have lived in a house that is thought to have had a 'presence,' but we have never been aware of a ghost down by the river. However it does have a sad legend that might have produced a 'presence'. One hot summers day, probably in the 1880s, when two farm labourers and their young families lived in The Cottage, the men returned home from the harvest field hot and sticky, and went for a swim in The Creek to cool off. On the first of the ebb, when the tide is running hard, a whirlpool forms off The Creek and when one of them reached this he sadly got into difficulties and drowned. Our home must have been the scene of terrible sadness.

The dust from the fireplace continued to fly. The horrid 1964 stove came out first and behind that were the remains of the 1947 cooker it had replaced. A Victorian halfpenny was found and James started bashing down a wall to get back to the original early seventeenth century fireplace. The investigation started to become interesting because one corner had been round where it would normally have been square. When all the rubble was cleared away there was a brick circle in the original floor of the fireplace.

'It is a well top,' suggested James ' but why indoors?'

Some old farmhouses had a well in the kitchen, but our well, which goes down below sea level, is just outside the back door. The old well builders were highly skilled and well paid. They started by building a circle of bricks on the ground and as the labourers dug out underneath the bricks slowly sank. They kept adding to the top of the circle of bricks until they reached water.

We sat and looked at the strange brick circle. The theory of a witch's cauldron was ruled out fairly quickly. Then came a smuggler's passage. There is also a story passed down among the older families in Alderton that horses used to come up the Beach Lane at night, loaded with smuggled goods landed in Hollesley Bay. Presumably this was stored in the smuggler's passage linking the church and the nearby farmhouse. Just across the river at Hemley Hall the farmer used to go into the stables in the morning and find his horses sweating because the smugglers had used them during the night. A bottle of Dutch gin would have been his part of the deal. In the eighteenth century there must have been some well-organized gangs operating in this area, but I only know of one recorded incident.

In 1778 the Revenue cutter *Bee,* commanded by Edward Hart, cruising in the Swin, spotted a known smuggling cutter commanded by 'one Cocks or Cox known as Horny Cock'. Sounds like a fun guy. The *Bee* chased the smuggling cutter to Orfordness where another smuggling cutter, with mounted guns, appeared. Faced with a superior force the Bee retreated sharply to Harwich. Guessing these smuggling cutters were about to 'run their contraband' Hart went out with fourteen men in his boats.

They soon found a forty-foot galley rowed by twelve oars, but it was empty. Our parish must have been a known place for smugglers because Hart and his party went there next. They found cart tracks going across the fields and these led to an underground cache, containing thirty-three half ankers of spirits. However before Hart could get the spirits back to his boats 'a hundred armed men' appeared and drove them away.

In the late eighteenth century the Suffolk coast was a virtual battleground between the smuggling gangs and the under-funded Revenue Service. It is reasonable to suppose that the people living in our Cottage would have know all about this incident and probably been part of it. Perhaps on dark winter evenings, decades later, the old men may have sat round our fireplace retelling the tale of the day they drove off the Revenue Men. Unfortunately I have never found any clues as to where the 'underground cache' had been, but there could well have been smuggler's hiding holes in any of the cottages.

James hammered out a section of the circle and found dirty sand underneath. Then I remembered the visit by Miss Butler, thirty years before, when she said this room had been the washhouse, but their copper had been in the far corner of that room. In the farmhouse where I grew up there were two coppers in The Back Kitchen. Both were great vats in which clothes were boiled to clean them. I never saw the big one, about five feet across the top, in use, but every Monday morning the fire was lit under the little one. While the water boiled, steam escaped from the wooden lid and turned the whole room into a Turkish bath. Could this brick circle in our house have been an earlier nineteenth century copper?

Paula, who comes to help Pearl, said she liked the more exciting explanation. Pity hadn't been a witch's cauldron or even the smugglers passage. To be honest we will nev know for certain, and the new stove covered up the evidence. This generated warmth unexpected ways, having to smash up wood in the shed, carrying in firewood and cleari up the everlasting dust. Pearl and I would not have had time to have done all this when carried the full weight of administration of the farming business. There is a price to pay working from home. From first thing in the morning until late at night the phone nev seemed to stop ringing. I really enjoyed the challenge, but I love the silence now it h stopped. Having handed over the everyday responsibility to Jonathan, his mobile nev stops ringing when we go sailing. When I had *L'Atalanta* one of the attractions was that could get away from the phone. Now I have a mobile, but sometimes leave it switched c There is no point in growing older if you don't grow a little wiser.

Perhaps being able to sit beside a wood fire prompted the idea of comfortable new cha to celebrate being married, and remaining in the same house for forty-five years. V travelled to central Suffolk where at Rendham we met Albert Lain, a former teacher who

Albert Lain, Pearl and craftsman Andrew Smith, with the Mendlesham chairs made with yew and elm.

persuasive salesmanship has worked up a considerable fine wood working business at the back of his house. He showed us his workshop and vegetable garden, of which he was rightly proud. Beyond it was the open country of wide-open fields of wheat and rape, dotted with oak trees and pig farms. We told him we would like two Mendlesham chairs made to celebrate forty-five years of marriage. Albert suggested that this length of permanent union ' must be as rare now-a-days as growing your own vegetables.'

It had stopped raining and the dog kept jumping up to show us that she wanted to go for a walk. Outside the river was still, the great bend sweeping around past the creek was completely empty of yachts, while off The Creek the natural white foam marked the ebb tide whirlpool. Out on the ooze little groups of waders were feeding and near the saltings were fresh otter tracks.

Following the footpath along the river wall path the marshland gave way to arable land and young trees on the edge of reed beds. There were no old trees because the salt water of the 1953 Floods killed them and the whole area had been altered with bulldozers and draglines. The delf ditch behind the wall had been moved further inland and river wall made higher, twice. Yet in spite of this human activity the area looks entirely natural. Nature is a very powerful force and when no management is done it automatically reverts to a wild state. The wind stirred the small branches of a young oak, a tree that had grown up since 1953. It was already about 30ft high, a height it would have reached since we came to live in The Cottage. Its growth marks the passage of time. In the summer the river is usually a peaceful place but in the winter it is often totally different and wild. The rain started again and a cold south-westerly wind blew up the empty river so I turned and walked home quickly. Life here is ruled by the weather and the tide.

Also from Creekside Publishing by Robert Simper.

English Estuaries Series

THE DEBEN RIVER
RIVER ORWELL AND RIVER STOUR
RIVERS ALDE, ORE AND BLYTH
NORFOLK RIVERS AND HARBOURS
ESSEX RIVERS AND CREEKS
THAMES TIDEWAY
RIVER MEDWAY AND THE SWALE
RIVERS TO THE FENS

The Sea and the Land books

IN SEARCH OF SAIL
FAMILY FIELDS
VOYAGE AROUND EAST ANGLIA
WOODBRIDGE & BEYOND

The Coast in the Past Series

FORGOTTEN COAST
SUNRISE COAST
THE LUGGER COAST